NEW DIRECTIONS FOR YOUTH DEVELOPMENT

Theory
Practicle
Research

winter | 2013

Innovations in Improving Access to Higher Education

Barbara Schneider
Justina Judy

issue
editors

Gil G. Noam
Editor-in-Chief

INNOVATIONS IN IMPROVING ACCESS TO HIGHER EDUCATION
Barbara Schneider, Justina Judy (editors)
New Directions for Youth Development, No. 140, Winter 2013
Gil G. Noam, Editor-in-Chief
This is a peer-reviewed journal.

Microfilm copies of issues and articles are available in 16mm and 35mm, as well as microfiche in 105mm, through University Microfilms Inc., 300 North Zeeb Road, Ann Arbor, MI 48106-1346.

New Directions for Youth Development is indexed in Academic Search (EBSCO), Academic Search Premier (EBSCO), Contents Pages in Education (T&F), Current Abstracts (EBSCO), Educational Research Abstracts Online (T&F), EMBASE/Excerpta Medica (Elsevier), ERIC Database (Education Resources Information Center), Index Medicus/MEDLINE/PubMed (NLM), MEDLINE/PubMed (NLM), SoclNDEX (EBSCO), Sociology of Education Abstracts (T&F), and Studies on Women & Gender Abstracts (T&F).

NEW DIRECTIONS FOR YOUTH DEVELOPMENT (ISSN 1533-8916, electronic ISSN 1537-5781) is part of the Jossey-Bass Psychology Series and is published quarterly by Wiley Subscription Services, Inc., A Wiley Company, at Jossey-Bass, One Montgomery Street, Suite 1200, San Francisco, CA 94104-4594. POSTMASTER: Send address changes to New Directions for Youth Development, Jossey-Bass, One Montgomery Street, Suite 1200, San Francisco, CA 94104-4594.

SUBSCRIPTIONS for individuals cost $89.00 for U.S./Canada/Mexico; $113.00 international. For institutions, agencies, and libraries, $318.00 U.S.; $358.00 Canada/Mexico; $392.00 international. Electronic only: $89.00 for individuals all regions; $318.00 for institutions all regions. Print and electronic: $98.00 for individuals in the U.S., Canada, and Mexico; $122.00 for individuals for the rest of the world; $366.00 for institutions in the U.S.; $406.00 for institutions in Canada and Mexico; $440.00 for institutions for the rest of the world. Prices subject to change. Refer to the order form that appears at the back of most volumes of this journal.

EDITORIAL CORRESPONDENCE should be sent to the Editor-in-Chief, Dr. Gil G. Noam, McLean Hospital, Harvard Medical School, 115 Mill Street, Belmont, MA 02478.

Cover photograph by © iStockphoto.com/Lisa Klumpp

www.josseybass.com

Contents

Issue Editors' Notes *1*
  Barbara Schneider, Justina Judy

Executive Summary *5*

1. Pathways to college and STEM careers: Enhancing the high school experience
   Barbara Schneider, Michael Broda, Justina Judy, Kri Burkander *9*

   This university-community partnership providing college mentoring and additional supports is having an impact on college-going rates and STEM interest in postsecondary education.

2. Research into practice: Postsecondary success in the Chicago Public Schools
   David W. Johnson, Eliza Moeller, Mathew Holsapple *31*

   A five-tenet framework guides the work of the Consortium on Chicago School Research in understanding and ameliorating the challenges facing low-income youth as they encounter the transition to college.

3. Lessons learned from a data-driven college access program: The National College Advising Corps
   Eileen L. Horng, Brent J. Evans, anthony l. antonio, Jesse D. Foster, Hoori S. Kalamkarian, Nicole F. Hurd, Eric P. Bettinger *55*

   A successful data-driven partnership between researchers at Stanford University and the National College Advising Corps has facilitated improved college access for low-income students.

4. The not-so-lazy days of summer: Experimental interventions to increase college entry among low-income high school graduates
   Benjamin L. Castleman, Lindsay C. Page *77*

   Peer mentoring and text messaging programs are shown to be helpful and cost-effective strategies for addressing the phenomenon of "summer melt" observed among low-income college-bound students.

5. Is traditional financial aid too little, too late to help youth
succeed in college? An introduction to *The Degree Project*
promise scholarship experiment
Douglas N. Harris   *99*
Promise scholarships, such as *The Degree Project*, offer an alternative to
traditional aid programs by making commitments to students early on in
high school and providing motivation and encouragement as students
prepare for college.

Index   *117*

Issue Editors' Notes

INCREASING ACCESS TO and persistence in college is one of the critical issues in education today and presents multiple challenges for secondary schools for how to prepare and support their students to navigate this increasingly complex process. There are a growing number of interventions designed to improve college access and matriculation for high school students; this is particularly the case for low-income families and first-generation college-goers as many are at risk for not attending college. Gaining an understanding about the barriers facing the transition from high school to college is a crucial step. These obstacles include a multitude of factors—lack of access to resources at home or school, not having a rigorous college-preparatory curriculum or not taking advantage of these courses when available, and misperceptions or faulty information about the college-going process.

In putting together this issue, we contacted scholars who not only conduct rigorous evaluations of interventions to improve the college-going process but also are at the forefront of developing innovative and effective ways to ease the transition process. One essential question raised by the contributors is the role of the high school. There is considerable attention regarding whether high schools should take a more active role than they currently do in preparing students for college. In response to this question, various experiments have been implemented in high schools that are designed to assist adolescents in forming their future plans after high school and complete the necessary steps to continue their education after graduation. Some of these experiments include large institutional initiatives that involve restructuring schools to become more college focused; others are smaller interventions that provide information, strengthen ties with parents, assist in the application process to college including financial aid, and promote strategic planning. While some of the interventions in this issue are designed for school-wide implementation, others are more targeted interventions that focus on one aspect of the college process, such as financial aid, but all recognize the role of high schools in shaping students' college-going aspirations and behavior.

Research demonstrates that increasing the college-going culture within a school through behavior, such as having high educational expectations for students, creating aligned ambitions, and enrolling in rigorous academic courses that are prerequisites for college admission, can make a difference in postsecondary enrollment. Schneider, Broda, Judy, and Burkander discuss specific ways high schools can develop and sustain a college-going culture. Horng, Evans, antonio, Foster, Kalamkarian, Hurd, and Bettinger describe how college advisers can work within schools to improve the college-going culture, focusing on the role of both qualitative and quantitative research in understanding the impact of the college-going culture on aspirations and college-going rates. Johnson, Moeller, and Holsapple reflect on how institutions, such as the Consortium on Chicago School Research, can create and maintain effective structures that support a college-going culture through networks of adult relationships in schools and connections between educators and young people. Interventions focusing more narrowly on one aspect of the college-going process, as discussed by Harris, still acknowledge the importance of creating a strong college-going culture in high schools.

Establishing and maintaining partnerships across institutions and among community stakeholders can provide a wealth of resources and information to support students through the college-going process. Johnson, Moeller, and Holsapple provide ways to develop and strengthen ongoing relationships between researchers and practitioners that support a strong network that facilitates the sharing of resources. In their evaluation of The National College Advising Corps, Horng, Evans, antonio, Foster, Kalamkarian, Hurd, and Bettinger explain how the intervention itself relies on

NEW DIRECTIONS FOR YOUTH DEVELOPMENT • DOI: 10.1002.yd

institutional partnerships between universities and local districts. The need for these institutional partnerships that can bridge secondary and postsecondary institutions is perhaps critically evident when addressing how to support students in the summer between completing high school and enrolling in college. As Castleman and Page describe in their work examining the obstacles of college enrollment and interventions to help mitigate attrition that occurs over the summer. Using college-going resources already available in the community and strengthening relationships between these resources is also a low-cost and sustainable strategy to improve access as discussed by Schneider, Broda, Judy, and Burkander.

One essential consideration in the evaluation of interventions mentioned by Horng and colleagues as well as Johnson, Moeller, and Holsapple is a discussion of how to handle negative findings, particularly when interventions are the result of university–community partnerships. It is vital, as a community of scholars, to be transparent with our data and results—whether positive or negative—since there are opportunities to learn from both outcomes.

This volume includes some of the most cutting-edge and rigorous research on improving college access and it is our goal that this issue helps to delineate the obstacles adolescents face in their transition from high school to college, increase our understanding of the mechanisms contributing to gaps in college enrollment, and highlight how interventions can help to ease these challenges.

We thank each of our colleagues who contributed to this volume as well as the administrative support received from Michelle Chester and Colleen Skelton at Michigan State University. We would also like to thank the students who gave their time and honestly opened up to researchers. This work would also not be possible without great schools across the country that open up their doors to partner with researchers in tackling these difficult issues of college access. Lastly, we thank the multiple sources of funding that supported the research in this volume including The National Science Foundation, National Institutes of Health, Institute for Educational Sciences, Bill and Melinda Gates Foundation, Spencer

Foundation, W. T. Grant Foundation, Heckscher Foundation for Children, Lindback Foundation, the National Association of Student Financial Aid Administers, and an anonymous donor. The opinions expressed here are those of the authors and do not necessarily reflect the positions of these funders.

Barbara Schneider
Justina Judy
Editors

BARBARA SCHNEIDER *is the John A. Hannah Chair and University Distinguished Professor at Michigan State University.*

JUSTINA JUDY *is a doctoral candidate in Educational Policy and Economics of Education Fellow at Michigan State University.*

Executive Summary

Chapter One: Pathways to college and STEM careers: Enhancing the high school experience

Barbara Schneider, Michael Broda, Justina Judy, Kri Burkander

With a rising demand for a college degree and an increasingly complicated college search, application, and selection process, there are a number of interventions designed to ease the college-going process for adolescents and their families. One such intervention, the College Ambition Program (CAP), is specifically designed to be a whole-school intervention that comprehensively connects several important aspects of the college-going process and specifically is focused on increasing interest in science, technology, engineering, and math (STEM). With many adolescents having interest in STEM careers but lacking knowledge of how to transform these interests into plans, CAP supports students in developing and pursuing their educational and occupational goals. CAP offers students tutoring and mentoring, course-counseling and advising, assistance through the financial aid process, and college experiences through visits to college campuses. In addition to these four core components, CAP is also pursuing how to integrate mobile technology and texting to further provide students with tailored resources and information about the college-going process. This chapter describes the complexities of the college-going process, the components of the CAP intervention, and presents findings that demonstrate that these strategies can increase college-going rates and interest in STEM. The authors highlight the importance of developing a college-going culture within high

NEW DIRECTIONS FOR YOUTH DEVELOPMENT, NO. 140, WINTER 2013 © WILEY PERIODICALS, INC.
Published online in Wiley Online Library (wileyonlinelibrary.com) • DOI: 10.1002/yd.20075

schools that support the alignment of postsecondary and career goals.

Chapter Two: Research into practice: Postsecondary success in the Chicago Public Schools

David W. Johnson, Eliza Moeller, Mathew Holsapple

In this chapter, the authors describe nearly a decade of research examining postsecondary outcomes of students in the Chicago Public Schools conducted by the Consortium on Chicago School Research (CCSR). These analyses include both long-term trends in college going and findings on the dimensions of students' postsecondary transition experiences that shape those outcomes. The authors describe the evolution of research at CCSR, which emphasizes a specific type of partnership between researchers, district officials, and practitioners that builds the capacity of practitioners and district officials to think critically about big problems and utilize data to inform decision-making and evaluation. In addition to describing these findings, the authors discuss the development and operation of the Network for College Success, a research-based, integrated and intensive support for school improvement to principals, their instructional leadership teams, grade level teams, and counselors. The authors describe how NCS builds the capacity of school leaders to work together and to use data to improve practice in the postsecondary transition. Finally, the authors discuss ongoing challenges and new directions for ongoing and future research.

Chapter Three: Lessons learned from a data-driven college access program: The National College Advising Corps

Eileen L. Horng, Brent J. Evans, anthony l. antonio, Jesse D. Foster, Hoori S. Kalamkarian, Nicole F. Hurd, Eric P. Bettinger

This chapter discusses the collaboration between a national college access program, the National College Advising Corps (NCAC), and its research and evaluation team at Stanford University. NCAC is currently active in almost four hundred high schools and through the placement of a recent college graduate to serve as a college adviser provides necessary information and support for students who may find it difficult to navigate the complex college admission process. The advisers also conduct outreach to underclassmen in an effort to improve the school-wide college-going culture. Analyses include examination of both quantitative and qualitative data from numerous sources and partners with every level of the organization from the national office to individual high schools. The authors discuss balancing the pursuit of evaluation goals with academic scholarship. In an effort to benefit other programs seeking to form successful data-driven interventions, the authors provide explicit examples of the partnership and present several examples of how the program has benefited from the data gathered by the evaluation team.

Chapter Four: The not-so-lazy days of summer: Experimental interventions to increase college entry among low-income high school graduates

Benjamin L. Castleman, Lindsay C. Page

Despite decades of policy intervention to increase college entry among low-income students, substantial inequalities in college going by family income remain. Policy makers have largely overlooked the summer after high school as an important time period in students' transition to college. During the post-high school summer, however, students must complete a range of financial and informational tasks prior to college enrollment, yet no longer have access to high school counselors and have not engaged yet with their college community. Moreover, many come from families with little college-going experience. Recent research documents summer attrition rates ranging from 10 to 40 percent among students who had been accepted to college and declared an intention to enroll in college as of high school graduation. Encouragingly, several experimental interventions demonstrate that students' postsecondary plans are quite responsive to additional outreach during the summer months. Questions nonetheless remain about how to maximize the impact and cost effectiveness of summer support. This chapter reports on several randomized trials to investigate the impact of summer counselor outreach and support as well as the potential roles for technology and peer mentoring in mitigating summer attrition and helping students enroll and succeed in college. The authors conclude with implications for policy and practice.

Chapter Five: Is traditional financial aid too little, too late to help youth succeed in college? An introduction to The Degree Project promise scholarship experiment

Douglas N. Harris

One of the key barriers in accessing postsecondary opportunities for many students is financial aid. This chapter begins by providing a review of prior evidence on the relationship between financial aid and postsecondary outcomes. One type of financial aid intervention that challenges traditional aid and scholarship options are "promise programs." These programs make commitments to low-income students when they are much younger than when students typically apply for aid and have the potential to encourage students to better prepare during high school, develop the social capital they need to navigate the path to college, and pay for growing college costs. In this chapter, the author describes the design and rationale for The Degree Project (TDP), which is the first randomized trial of a promise scholarship in the United States. In addition to the important new evidence the demonstration program will generate, TDP also shows how educators and researchers can work together to provide the insight and answers policy makers need to address very real education gaps.

NEW DIRECTIONS FOR YOUTH DEVELOPMENT • DOI: 10.1002.yd

High schools can create a college-going culture that helps students visualize themselves in college, create strategic plans for reaching their postsecondary aspirations, and support school personnel in making college a reality regardless of family income and other economic and social constraints.

1

Pathways to college and STEM careers: Enhancing the high school experience

Barbara Schneider, Michael Broda, Justina Judy, Kri Burkander

YOUNG CHILDREN DREAM of becoming firemen, doctors, and teachers; those in middle school imagine themselves as athletes, actors, and criminal investigators. By sophomore year in high school, the overwhelming majority of adolescents expect to attend college, often at elite institutions such as Harvard or Stanford University. Jobs become less defined as the choices for how to acquire them become more immediate. For many students, their dreams of attending highly competitive, expensive private schools are as unrealistic as becoming a movie actor or professional athlete. College ambitions are pervasive, and while some students may set their sights on public state schools or two-year institutions, the overwhelming majority expect to attain a four-year degree and this does not significantly vary by social and economic resources or race and ethnicity. Part of the lack of realism can be traced to the ubiquitous societal view on the importance of college and the lack of information on what it takes to be accepted at a college both in terms of academic preparation and economic and social resources. Applying to a college that matches students' interests, academic strengths and talents, and personal preferences, as well as family values and resources, is a complicated process.

Applying to and enrolling in postsecondary schools is challenging for all students and it can be especially difficult for low-income and first-generation college students.[1] Selecting the right college is a complex undertaking, where access to information and other resources exacerbates existing educational inequalities. High schools serving primarily middle- and high-income students have considerable resources to promote the college-going process and are supported in their efforts by teachers who are poised and parents who are tenacious in furthering postsecondary aspirations. The situation in high schools serving low-income populations, located in urban or rural areas, is quite different. Oftentimes, the schools do not have the resources to offer advanced level courses or college guidance services, and parent knowledge of the college application process and financial aid options is limited.

Recently, a number of interventions have been designed to learn how best to help low-income students enroll and persist in college. These efforts are different from prior programs in that they are targeted at those students whose academic skills and talents would be better matched with more competitive postsecondary institutions and include specific procedures for assisting in the college application process including financial aid options. One of these interventions is the College Ambition Program (CAP), which takes a somewhat broader approach, trying to change the high school culture into one where students not only talk about going to college but also learn more about what it takes to be a competitive applicant and how to match interests with postsecondary options. This chapter describes the intricacies of the college-going process, components of the CAP model, and its implementation, results, and sustainability.

NEW DIRECTIONS FOR YOUTH DEVELOPMENT • DOI: 10.1002.yd

The complexity of the college search process

The experiences of adolescents in high school often determine the trajectory of their academic preparation, educational expectations, and career knowledge—all of which are critical for achieving post-secondary success. Recognizing the importance of advanced academic courses critical for college preparation, many states have increased their high school graduation requirements in subjects like mathematics and science. High schools serving middle- and high-income students tended to offer these courses even before such requirements existed. Not only do these schools have experience offering such courses and teachers with expertise in these subjects, there is support for the students to receive extra help to succeed in these courses. Additionally, parents often hire tutors to assist students not only in remedial courses but also those in advanced levels. In schools serving low-income students, extra help to succeed in these types of college preparation courses is not available nor do parents have the resources to hire tutors. The challenge for the high school is how to offer additional help for these types of courses—which fall outside of the remedial curriculum and courses for students with special needs. Thus, the very first and key part of the college-going process is to encourage students to take advanced level courses and to provide them with the support to succeed in these courses.

In addition to the academic challenges of being prepared for college, there is the actual application process itself. This can be especially difficult both personally and institutionally. On the personal side, students may aspire to certain types of jobs but are unaware of how much education is needed to achieve their goals. Referred to as having unaligned ambitions, this is most common among those students whose parents have not attended postsecondary school, although students in middle- and upper-class families can also be misinformed and overestimate how much education is required for certain jobs. Having unaligned ambitions can affect the types of programs and institutions students are interested in attending.[2]

NEW DIRECTIONS FOR YOUTH DEVELOPMENT • DOI: 10.1002.yd

Another challenge for students (particularly low income and minority) is "undermatching," which is when students possess the necessary academic preparation to attend a more selective four-year institution, yet choose to attend a less-selective one and sometimes such institutions can end up being more expensive.[3] Research examining those students who are undermatched indicates that they are less likely than their peers to complete their degree on time and are more likely to drop out of college altogether.[4] One population that seems highly prone to undermatch are those high school students living in rural areas of the United States.[5]

On the institutional side, the process of seeking out, applying, and enrolling in college is increasing in complexity, driven in part by changes in university marketing and recruitment practices, and rising costs of college and institutional factors such as decreasing campus need-based aid.[6] The process of researching, planning, and preparing to go to college is one that requires years of careful consideration, years that need to start well before the senior year. In many high schools with higher than average college attendance numbers, the college selection process heats up in the end of sophomore year with notices of when and how to prepare for college entrance exams and the possibility of applying for early admission. The early admission process begins in earnest in the junior year. Without interventions earlier in the secondary school experience, by senior year, many students who try to begin the college search process can become overwhelmed and simply give up or take a path of least resistance and apply to a local two-year college.

For all students, selecting colleges that align with their interests, skills, and talents requires a strategic planning process that relies on knowledgeable family and school personnel who can provide requisite information for making sound postsecondary choices. As shown in Figure 1.1, Schneider & Stevenson outlined key steps in acquiring the knowledge, skills, and mindsets necessary to be successful in the college search.[7]

First, and perhaps most important, a student needs to visualize oneself as a college student. This means not only understanding what the college experience looks and feels like, but also being able

Figure 1.1. The college search: A theory of action

to place herself in the shoes of a college student—knowing something about what is expected, the courses one should take, and how to manage their time. Second, a student needs to transform that vision into realistic actions by making tangible connections to actions that can help reach their goal. This might entail taking more rigorous courses, becoming involved in extracurricular activities, or seeking out tutoring to become more proficient in a subject area. Finally, once seeing the connections between the vision of college enrollment and specific actions in high school, a student creates a plan for securing financial aid, navigating relevant deadlines, and settling on where to live and how to make that happen. Parent and family resources in more affluent communities frequently support this third step (often referred to as "helicopter" parents), which often involves specific logistical knowledge and resources including frequent trips to colleges and explicitly going over the details of the first few weeks of postsecondary school. In school contexts with fewer resources, creating strategic plans becomes a much more challenging process, and a student can easily become overwhelmed and unsure of what information is required—from filling out housing forms to understanding what is owed for tuition, and when that amount has to be paid.

Assisting high school students in the college application process

There are a number of interventions currently in place that have been specifically designed to assist low-income students in the college-going process. Some of these focus on completing financial aid forms, others on coaching and mentoring models. Without a doubt, certain key behaviors, such as completing the Free

Application for Federal Student Aid (FAFSA) form and submitting on-time college applications, serve as gatekeepers for enrollment. However, focusing exclusively on these tasks has the potential to encourage students to fill out applications for the sake of filling them out, without receiving the necessary mindset and support for following through to enrollment. This is not to say that an effective school-wide program should not focus on FAFSA or college applications; rather, a comprehensive program should attend to these gatekeeping steps as part of a larger spectrum of microlevel shifts in students' knowledge and attitudes toward college going.

In the past several years, funding and interest have increased in school-based models that place college advisors in low-income schools for a one- to two-year period.[8] The advisor, or "coach," model, functions somewhat akin to other education programs, such as Teach For America (TFA) and The Teaching Fellows (TF), which recruit high-performing, achievement-oriented recent college graduates, provide them with basic training and support, and then place them in high-needs schools. In the case of the National College Advising Corps (NCAC) and other coach models, advisors serve as college coaches, and work with seniors to fill out college applications and submit required financial aid forms. In many cases, coaches are affiliated with the school guidance staff in which they work and spend much of their time in one-on-one meetings with juniors and seniors. Coaches are an important part of developing and sustaining a college-going culture within a school while providing crucial services and support for students to attend college.

To be sure, there are certain advantages afforded by the coach model. For one, coaches tend to be young, driven, and often come from more diverse racial and socioeconomic backgrounds than most high school guidance staff. This could likely translate into strong relationships and trust between coaches and students, and encourage more students to follow their advice and apply for admission and aid. In addition, since most coaches tend to be recent college graduates, they are in a unique situation to mentor high school seniors, having just spent time in college and familiar with questions and apprehensions that seniors may have about beginning the process. This would likely improve the "take-up" of advice and counsel from coach to prospective student. College coaches are typically limited to a small set of college-related tasks, namely, working with upperclassmen to encourage filling out applications for admission and financial aid, as well as providing in-the-moment advice and mentoring during one-on-one sessions.

Supporting students in high school: The College Ambition Program

CAP is more holistic in its approach to college entrance and focuses not only on juniors and seniors, but is available to all students as the process begins well before the final two years of high school. Designed to promote a college-going culture in schools, CAP works to improve adolescents' understanding of the educational requirements for a given career path and assists students in developing the knowledge, attitudes, and behaviors to attain that goal. CAP includes four components: (1) tutoring and mentoring, (2) course counseling and advising, (3) financial aid planning and assistance, and (4) college experiences—visits to campuses. Leveraging near-age peers, low-cost mobile technology and texting, and university-based partnership, the CAP model not only supports the development of a college-going culture in high schools, but is built to be sustained by the school after the initial research/trial period ends.

Each of the four components primarily operates through a "CAP Center" that is open three days a week for six hours, including after school. This schedule is designed to be accessible to students while not disrupting class attendance during the day. The CAP Center is an integral part of the school rather than just a supplemental service. Announcements and signs are posted throughout the building, and CAP staff members are encouraged to make presentations in classes and attend school functions. Students are encouraged by their teachers and counselors to attend the Center for tutoring help and college preparation. A full-time CAP site co-ordinator organizes the mentors and other activities sponsored by CAP, including school-wide events and college visits.

CAP has developed an extensive set of activities, beginning when students first enter high school that helps them make more informed choices about courses and the steps for applying to different types of colleges. One programmatic aspect of CAP is to introduce students to colleges that have specialized programs in science, technology, engineering, and mathematics (STEM). Low-income and minority students are underrepresented in STEM fields. Colleges and employers are actively recruiting STEM college majors and projections by the Bureau of Labor Statistics and other federal agencies indicate that careers in STEM fields are likely to increase.[9]

Partnering with the schools' counseling staff, CAP staff advises students on selecting courses that align with particular careers of interest and curriculum requirements for their individual needs. CAP offers tutorial help using undergraduate students for subjects in which students often have demonstrated difficulty—algebra, statistics, biology, chemistry, physics, and English—all of which are important for college admissions and entrance exams. These near-age undergraduate tutors (often of like race and ethnicity) are clear role models of successful college students. Trained not only to complete homework assignments, the tutors are available during CAP hours as well as after school for help and advice. CAP has been successful in recruiting honors students from local undergraduate STEM programs, who describe their experiences as "an opportunity to give back," "a chance to help someone like me and the challenges I had," and "learning more about who I am and whether working in a school is a possibility for my future."

To address some of the financial pressures low-income families may face in paying for college, CAP has developed a series of materials that go beyond just assisting students through the FAFSA process. CAP supports students in searching for scholarships and additional grants, understanding how much money students are still responsible for after receiving scholarships and/or financial

NEW DIRECTIONS FOR YOUTH DEVELOPMENT • DOI: 10.1002.yd

aid, and what actionable steps students and their families need to complete between college acceptance and matriculation in the fall. For example, CAP helps students prepare for invitational interviews to prestigious four-year colleges, relying on the expertise of one of the CAP coordinators who had previously worked in college admissions at an elite university. Additionally, CAP has worked with the law school to assist parents with immigration problems and tax issues that could prevent their children from receiving federal financial aid.

Even when low-income students receive acceptance into college and financial aid, some still fail to matriculate in the fall. CAP intensively works with graduating seniors in May to identify how much money the family and the student needs to begin college in the fall, what health insurance and other forms must be completed, how to plan for living arrangements, how to register for classes, and how to seek employment (especially work-study opportunities).

CAP has also designed a special training program for students visiting campuses to assist them in evaluating how the college fits their expectations. In contrast to various other programs or interventions that might offer college visits oftentimes only to high performing students, CAP provides this opportunity to all students at no cost and takes advantage of local programs and foundations that can support the costs associated with each trip. Prior to each visit, students prepare in advance—learning what to look for at each campus and what questions to ask admissions representatives while on the visit. This has been a beneficial experience for many of the students who have never been on a college campus even though they may live only twenty minutes away. Responses from college visit evaluations indicate for some students the visit helped to shape their views on the type of campus where they would feel more "at home" and able to succeed.

Summer outreach

Even if students successfully navigate the college application and selection process during high school, the summer between their graduation and the start of college has been found to be a vulnerable time in which students who intend to enroll in college fail to actually matriculate.[10] This phenomenon is commonly referred to as "summer melt." (See Chapter 4 in this volume.) Based on the research of summer melt, in the spring of 2012, CAP extended its near-age mentoring to a subsample of randomly selected students in the intervention schools as well as in a sample of matched comparison schools. Before graduation, seniors in both CAP and matched comparison schools were asked to fill out an exit survey which included questions about their future plans (attend a university, college, community college, trade school, and so on) and general levels of comfort with the financial aid, registration, and orientation process. Students were also asked to provide multiple means of contact, such as a mobile phone number or an email address.

Selected students were assigned to one of a small group of summer mentors, made up of current undergraduates and graduate students working on campus in the summer. Some mentors worked with CAP during the school year and some responded to a posted announcement on a university-wide service learning job/volunteer board. Each mentor attended a two-hour training with a CAP staff member that covered several topics, including maintaining students' privacy and confidentiality, tips for mentoring adolescents, and a general background on the most common financial aid questions students might encounter. Following the templates created by Castleman et al., CAP developed a series of contact protocols tailored to specific issues and modes of interaction.[11] These included an initial "intake" interview template and several different follow-up protocols for providing more in-depth assistance. One key finding coming out of the summer work was that text messaging serves as a low cost and efficient means of encouraging participation in CAP interventions. Our take-up rates were very close to the rate reported by Castleman et al., with nearly 60 percent of students responding to text message outreach.[12] Take-up rates for email contact were much lower, at about 20 percent.

Reinforced by the need to reach students both in and out of school and the initial success of summer mentoring through texting support, in the 2012–2013 school year CAP implemented a randomized "microintervention." This randomized within-school study allows for more accurate estimation of program effects at the student level as well as reaching more students through a more innovative medium—their cell phone. Advances in smartphone and mobile application (app) technology provide new ways for outreach, especially for adolescents. Using smartphones not only can expand the extent to which information and resources can reach students but it also can provide students with direct interaction and opportunities for obtaining follow-up information from the services.

The use of smartphones in education is also growing among the adolescent population, even those students from low-income households, with approximately one in three students using their phones for help on homework.[13] Growth can also be seen in smartphone companies that spend an estimated $20 billion a year on research and development. Contrast that to the annual spending of the National Science Foundation, around $250 million, it is evident that the ability to use smartphones to support students transitioning to adulthood is not only cutting edge, but is quickly becoming a necessity.

The microintervention experiment intended to provide data for measuring the effects by generating random variation in student participation in CAP through the use of a targeted "nudge." Rather than directly assigning students to receive the CAP treatment, the probability that a random student takes the treatment is encouraged through the nudge text message with information or upcoming deadlines. This generates experimental-type conditions, but where conducting a randomized experiment is not a possibility (for example, limiting CAP services to a random sample of students within a high school).[14] The strength of the encouragement is hypothesized to be driven by simple changes in students' "default behaviors," a concept which has been used to more generally motivate another college access intervention.[15] In this context, the default behavior of most students is not to employ an available resource for college access (for example, the CAP center) that is nearly costless to the student and potentially quite beneficial.

The text messages were sent between 3:30 p.m. and 4:00 p.m. on three consecutive Mondays in the month of February. Each week, the text message highlighted a different aspect of CAP services, including help with college applications, filling out the FAFSA, and searching for scholarships and awards to reduce the cost of attendance. The full text of each message is below. (Note: each message is customized to match school characteristics, such as CAP center location, and so on.)

Week One: It's not too late to apply for college! Most schools accept applications until March 1st or even later. Stop by CAP in Rm 305 today to get application help.

Week Two: Worried about paying for college? You could qualify for up to half off your college tuition. Stop by CAP in Rm 305 today to learn more about financial aid.

Week Three: Need help finding scholarships for college? Not sure where to look? The CAP Center in Rm 305 can help you find extra money for college. Stop by soon!

The research utilizing text messaging as part of CAP is preliminary and ongoing, but we expect that this will be a cost effective and efficient means of boosting CAP participation in treatment schools. More importantly, it provides within school randomized estimates of take-up. Based on results from first year of the nudge experiment, we find among those students who received the nudge compared to students who did not that the treated were more likely to visit the CAP center ($t = 19$, $p < .0001$). Given the relatively low cost of the intervention (about $6 per student), the limited labor required, and its ability to reach students personally, we are optimistic that this design will be useful in a larger set of treatment schools and as a practical way to get students knowledge and helpful information.

NEW DIRECTIONS FOR YOUTH DEVELOPMENT • DOI: 10.1002.yd

Preliminary findings

To measure the impact of CAP on college going, multiple measures were created and obtained from student, mentor, and teacher surveys, CAP coordinator logs and sign-in data, and intensive interviews with students, teachers, and other school staff. Items on CAP student questionnaires were drawn from national student surveys, which facilitate comparison of CAP survey data with nationally representative samples. Survey measures included items on postsecondary expectations, college ambition, perceptions of college cost, financial aid, various actors' influence on the college planning/application process, students' math and science perceptions, and demographic variables of interest. College enrollment and choice of major data are obtained from the senior exit survey. The CAP data are also augmented with additional data from school administrative records. After three years, the following briefly describes the first set of findings, from analyses of the surveys and interviews.

Student responses on surveys merged with state data were analyzed using several statistical procedures. The following results are based on six high schools in mid-Michigan that participated as either a treatment or a control school. Using pre- and postsurvey data from high school seniors in both treatment and control schools, the analysis examines the impact of the CAP intervention on seniors' intent to enroll in postsecondary institution immediately after their high school graduation. This impact analysis employs logistic regression to measure several potential postsecondary intentions taken in the senior year including no college, attendance at a two-year college, and attendance at a four-year college and their eventual destinations fall 2012.[16] Results from these inferential statistics indicate that among those students who participated in CAP in the first three years, students in urban schools were significantly less likely to expect to attend a four-year college compared to their counterparts in the rural schools; on average, urban students were 21 percentage points lower than rural students in their expectations. Minority students were also significantly less likely to expect to attend a four-year college, with a predicted probability 7 percentage points lower than nonminority students.

Consistent with previous research, males are more likely than females to pursue a degree in STEM; in our sample the predicted probability for males to be interested in a STEM major was 13.5 percentage points higher than the females. There was a difference between urban and rural schools in STEM major as well; the predicted probability for urban schools was 4 percentage points higher than rural schools. Examining the differences between the treatment and control schools, students in the treatment schools were more likely to show interest in pursuing a STEM major, with a difference in predicted probability of 5.7 percentage points.

A preliminary analysis of actual postsecondary enrollment rates with a partial sample of treatment schools shows a positive and significant treatment effect on all postsecondary enrollment ($t = 29.90$, $p < .0001$). The sample for this statistical analysis included a large sample ($n > 1,000$) of students in both treatment and control groups and made use of actual postsecondary enrollment data from 2006–2007 to 2010–2011. These results are consistent with prior simulation estimates using propensity-matching techniques with large national datasets.[17] While we are encouraged by these results, they are still preliminary and do not meet the conditions by which one could estimate a causal link between treatment and enrollment. As we continue to add treatment schools and expand our control sample, we will further systematically and rigorously examine this relationship.

Student perspectives

In summer 2012, intensive qualitative interviews were conducted with a randomly selected group of seniors regarding their plans for the fall, what they were doing over the summer, and their expectations and concerns about graduating high school and entering college.[18] These interviews provide a rich source of data that highlights the development and familial resources these students face, in combination with institutional, school-related problems.

Preliminary findings point to issues of individuation and independence (that is, the developmental process of young adults including their self-concept, sense of responsibilities, and behaviors) in leaving home for college.[19] Leaving home for college raises concerns among students even if they plan on living at home while attending community college.

One of the overriding themes from the interviews indicate that familial and parental support, often conceived of as a universal asset to developing college ambition, appears to function in highly complex ways in students' lives. For example, there seems to be a difference between parental support in urban and rural families, where parental support in urban contexts encourages students to go out on their own, while parental support in rural contexts tends to encourage students to stay close to home for a longer period. The following quotes extracted from some of the interviews transcribed and coded for issues of self-esteem, independence, and strategic planning underscore these differences and illustrate how students' development and familial resources interact with the school and academic context in transitioning from high school to college.

Miranda lives in a rural community and plans to pursue a career in the medical field. At first she thought about attending a four-year college but she worried that she was not ready for such a big transition. Her family is supporting her to attend a two-year college and live at home. "My parents wanted me to go to college and pushed that. I've talked to people older than me at CAP lab and stuff and I said my parents always pushed me to go. One student in the CAP center said, 'Oh, my parents never did, that wasn't even talked about.' That was shocking to me, because my parents have always pushed that." However, when it came time to complete the FAFSA, Miranda received less support. "My mom was really upset. She actually did a lot of it. She said if you don't get anything from this then I'm not doing it again. I know they want you to do it every single year, but if you don't benefit from it then why am I going to waste my time."

Helen also lives in a rural area and plans to attend a four-year college in the fall. She discusses the lack of college resources in her life: "I don't really talk to many people who have gone to college. I don't get a chance to really talk to them. Because I'm not close enough to them to even care to ask. And I don't want to get all personal with somebody if they're not like a close friend. I don't want to pry into their life or anything. So I usually just let it go." She describes the resistance she faced from her aunt, who suggested that she pursue a two-year degree rather than attend a university. "[She] was all like 'you couldn't afford university anyways so you might as well just go to [community college]' but Helen resolved, "I'm not going to let my financial situation hold me back from doing what I want to do." She further explains the challenges of talking with her mother, who did not attend any postsecondary school. "She is hard to have a conversation with. She doesn't understand anything." Instead Helen has turned for help from a friend's parent, "My best friend, Allie…her mom has helped me out a lot. Looking at all my stuff and showing me how to do everything. She helped me with the housing because she helped Allie do hers. These people are the ones that help me out…the ones that know what to do. My mom is kind of clueless."

While the familial support may differ by context, both rural and urban first-generation students faced challenges in accessing the necessary information and resources. One urban two-year college-bound student, Sarafina, describes getting advice from others she knew, "And I was thinking to myself one day, well, how am I supposed to do all of this and college? And so I would ask other college students, [and] my sisters, because I trust them, and they're all, 'Oh no, it's fine. You're only going into class for a couple of hours for maybe one or two days a week', and it's like, 'Ok, if you say so.'" She explains that she got information from counselors at school because, as a first-generation student, "My parents couldn't really talk about it."

Compared to the rural schools, the urban ones have more access to more resources, courses, and college-preparation materials. Sarafina describes the college preparation she received as a part of the International Baccalaureate Program (IB) at her school, "The IB teachers they say over and over and over again, more than any other teachers. This is a syllabus, this is what it's going to be like in college; you might want to keep up."

Helen (see above) on the other hand, discusses her frustration with the lack of adequate academic challenge and college preparation at her school. She compares her public school with the local Catholic school, explaining that the teachers have high standards and that the students there have higher test scores as a result. "We are just kind of like–left. I don't think they did enough for us. I think they could have done more especially preparing us for college. We only offer two AP classes, AP biology and AP English. I didn't do those. I took CP (college prep) English and even that was still a joke. Like, there was nothing college prep about it; our papers were worth ten points."

Friends and peers appear to help one another contributing to the college-going attitudes and behaviors of each other. John, a rural student intending to transfer to a four-year college after starting at a community college, describes the way his friends supported each other to pursue their college goals, "They have similar goals, going for four-year degrees, or maybe a little more afterwards … Everybody is in the same boat asking questions senior year, 'Where are you going to college? Do you think it's going to be hard' kind of questions. Everyone is working on each other." An urban four-year college-bound student, Lloyd, describes the pressure he felt from his peers in honors classes to follow a similar path to college. "I take a lot of honors classes so most of the people in my classes are college bound. So I mean, I think they have influenced me a lot as far as the want to get good grades and the want to go to college and I mean everybody else around me is doing it, shoot, end up the only one not doing it."

An urban two-year college-bound student, Brittany, describes the college press among her peers. "We always talked about college since we were freshman in high school. 'What are you going to do? Where are you going to be?' Like we were little kids still. 'When I grow up I want to be this that and the other.' So my friends and I, we stayed on track together. We always helped each other study. We always helped each other with homework. Sometimes we didn't

do homework, but we said, 'Girl, we got to get that work done!'"
Even when she had a baby in the middle of her junior year, her
friends provided support to help her keep up. They would say, "'If
you need me to watch him so you can get something done, I'll do
it.' They were more than 'let me be there for you' and I was like,
Ok. So my friends influenced me by making sure I stayed on task
and 'do you need help with your homework' 'did you get what you
missed when you had Jay?' I got it. Thanks everybody. My friends
are good."

Sustainability, policy, and practical applications

CAP is specifically designed for low-income public high schools
and seeks to operate at a relatively small price tag so that the
lessons learned can be modeled into existing programs. One consideration for new intervention programs like CAP is to plan how
to make these programs sustainable beyond two or three years—
specifically, how to access and train human and intellectual resources in the school that can take over the school-wide intervention. One possible idea is to leverage younger teachers in the
building who may be pursuing advanced degrees in educational
leadership (required to become a building principal or district ad-
ministrator). Most degree programs require teachers to take on a
specific leadership role often focused on reaching struggling students. Another idea is to include time in the CAP center as part
of the internship experience for beginning high school teachers.
In the future, CAP will be working with the secondary teacher
education program to determine if the training of high school
teachers can incorporate such experiences into their programmatic
requirements.

As the demand for a college-educated population increases,
so have the numbers of interventions, many of which include components, such as training for counselors to improve
their college counseling expertise, offering schools tutoring and
mentoring staff, providing information and assisting students with
filling out financial aid forms, and taking students on college visits.

NEW DIRECTIONS FOR YOUTH DEVELOPMENT • DOI: 10.1002.yd

While helpful, these interventions typically focus on one aspect of the college-going process, and few deliver training for accessing and using the information that many parents and students need to understand the material they receive. In contrast to these one-dimensional reforms, CAP is specifically designed to be an intervention that comprehensively connects several important aspects of the college-going process. Extending support services to students through the use of text messaging as well over the summer through simple, cost-effective outreach might further increase the likelihood of students successfully fulfilling their postsecondary aspirations. The process of navigating the myriad challenges students face on the road to college enrollment cannot be solved by interventions that focus support on the senior year. Rather, a truly comprehensive approach must meet students in all grades (9–12) where they are, and begin to build skills and mindsets to smooth the process as they grow older. A fixation on the gatekeepers of college going ignores the many challenges low-income students face along the way, leading many to arrive at the gate, but far fewer to walk through.

Notes

1. Hoxby, C., & Avery, C. (2012). *The missing "One-Offs": The hidden supply of high-achieving, low income students* (NBER Working Paper 18586). Cambridge, MA: National Bureau of Economic Research; Hoxby, C., & Turner, S. (2013). *Expanding college opportunities for high-achieving, low income students* (SIEPR Discussion Paper No. 12–014). Stanford, CA: Stanford Institute for Economic Policy Research.

2. Schneider, B., & Stevenson, D. (1999). *The ambitious generation: America's teenagers, motivated but directionless*. New Haven, CT: Yale University Press.

3. Roderick, M., Coca, V., & Nagaoka, J. (2011). Potholes on the road to college: High school effects in shaping urban students' participation in college application, four-year college enrollment, and college match. *Sociology of Education, 84*, 178–211; Smith, J., Pender, M., & Howell, J. (2013). The full extent of student-college academic undermatch. *Economics of Education Review, 32*, 247–261.

4. Bowen, W., Chingos, M., & McPherson, M. (2009). *Crossing the finish line: Completing college at America's public universities*. Princeton, NJ: Princeton University Press.

5. Hoxby & Avery (2012); Smith, J., Pender, M., & Howell, J. (2012). *The full extent of student-college academic undermatch.* The College Board Advisory and Policy Center; Schneider, B., Broda, M., & Judy, J. (2013). *Improving postsecondary outcomes for low-income students.* Paper presented at the Society for Research on Education Effectiveness (SREE) Spring 2013 Conference, Washington, DC.

6. Kinzie, J., Palmer, M., Hayek, J., Hossler, D., Jacob, S. A., & Cummings, H. (2004). *Fifty years of college choice: Social, political and institutional influences on the decision-making process* (Vol. 5, No. 3). Indianapolis, IN: Lumina Foundation for Education.

7. Schneider & Stevenson (1999).

8. See the National College Advising Corps (http://www.advisingcorps. org), and local- and state-level affiliates.

9. Bureau of Labor Statistics (BLS). (2009). *Employment projections: 2008–2018 summary.* Retrieved October 20, 2011, from http://www.bls. gov/news.release/archives/ecopro_12102009.htm; National Science Board (NSB). (2010). *Preparing the next generation of STEM innovators: Identifying and developing our nation's human capital.* Arlington, VA: Author.

10. Arnold, K. D., Fleming, S., DeAnda, M. A., Castleman, B. L., Wartman, K. L., & Price, P. (2009). The summer flood: The invisible gap among low-income students. *Thought and Action, Fall,* 23–34; Castleman, B. L., Arnold, K. D., & Wartman, K. L. (2012). Stemming the tide of summer melt: An experimental study of the effect of post-high school summer intervention on low-income students' college enrollment. *The Journal of Research on Educational Effectiveness, 5*(1), 1–18.

11. Castleman et al. (2012).

12. Castleman et al. (2012); The data needed to make this inference is not available yet. In summer 2013, we expect to receive outcome data from the State of Michigan via the National Student Clearinghouse.

13. Khadaroo, S. T. (2012). Not just 4 texting: 1 in 3 middle-schoolers uses smart phones for homework. *The Christian Science Monitor.* Retrieved from http://www.csmonitor.com/USA/Education/2012/1129/Not-just-4-texting-1-in-3-middle-schoolers-uses-smart-phones-for-homework

14. Frangakis, C., Rubin, D., & Zhou, X-H. (2004). Clustered encouragement design with individual noncompliance: Bayesian inference and application to Advance Directive Forms. *Biostatistics, 3*(2), 147–164.

15. Carrell, S., & Sacerdote, B. (2012). *Late interventions matter too: The case of college coaching in New Hampshire.* Cambridge, MA: National Bureau of Economic Research.

16. Data used in this analysis are restricted to students in the 12th grade during the 2010–2011 and 2011–2012 school year. This sample included a total of 1,070 12th grade students from the treatment and control high schools. The survey response rate across the schools was 80 percent.

17. Schneider, B., Khawand, C., & Judy, J. (March 2012). *The College Ambition Program: Improving opportunities for High School Students Transitioning to College.* Paper presented at the spring conference of the Society for Research on Educational Effectiveness, Washington, DC.

18. Burkander, K. (2013). *Ambition in transition: Voices from rural and urban students regarding the transition from high school to college.* Manuscript in preparation.

19. Erikson, E. H. (1968). *Identity, youth, and crisis.* New York: W. W. Norton & Company; Blos, P. (1967). The second individuation process of adolescence. *Psychoanalytic Study of the Child, 22,* 162–186.

BARBARA SCHNEIDER *is the John A. Hannah Chair and University Distinguished Professor at Michigan State University.*

MICHAEL BRODA *is a University Distinguished Fellow at Michigan State University.*

JUSTINA JUDY *is a doctoral candidate in Educational Policy and Economics of Education Fellow at Michigan State University.*

KRI BURKANDER *is a doctoral candidate in Educational Policy at Michigan State University.*

This chapter describes the five-tenet framework that guides the work of the Consortium on Chicago School Research in understanding and ameliorating the challenges facing low-income youth as they encounter the transition to college.

2

Research into practice: Postsecondary success in the Chicago Public Schools

David W. Johnson,
Eliza Moeller, Mathew Holsapple

EDUCATIONAL ATTAINMENT AND social inequality are strongly related to one another in the United States. There are durable historical links between the highest level of education a person achieves, their own individual economic productivity, and aggregate national economic growth, especially during the twentieth century.[1] Economic restructuring in the twenty-first century has only reinforced the links between educational attainment and economic (in)security. In the starkest terms, the global economy of the twenty-first century holds little promise for youth who do not complete some form of postsecondary education or job training.[2] A recent report by researchers at the Consortium on Chicago School Research (CCSR) highlights this issue in Chicago finding that nearly half of Chicago Public Schools (CPS) graduates in a given year finish high school with such low grades and test scores that they have no access to four-year colleges.[3] Often finding themselves completely out of both the labor market and postsecondary education in the year

NEW DIRECTIONS FOR YOUTH DEVELOPMENT, NO. 140, WINTER 2013 © WILEY PERIODICALS, INC.
Published online in Wiley Online Library (wileyonlinelibrary.com) • DOI: 10.1002/yd.20077

after graduation, the prognosis for these students is dire: without substantial intervention, many will never earn a living wage, while still others may never work consistently at all.

For the CPS graduates—and the thousands of students like them across the country whose grades and test scores give them access to a range of four-year college options—the outlook is somewhat more positive, if not less complicated. For these students, recent national research suggests that college completion, not college access, may be the more critical challenge for American youth. In an analysis of data from the *Current Population Survey*, Bowen, Chingos, and McPherson observe that a decades-long trend of rising educational attainment in the United States essentially stalled and reversed in the mid-1970s.[4] In the forty years since, while larger and larger numbers of young people have enrolled in college, the proportion who complete college degrees has remained essentially the same.[5] The length of time it takes students to complete degrees has also risen over this period and this increase has been most acute at the less selective institutions most likely to serve urban and minority students.[6] This suggests that while access to college remains a pressing problem for many more students nationally, the challenge has become not just getting in, but getting through college.

The problem of low postsecondary attainment for urban students is one of the most pressing concerns for the field of youth development. The strong connection between educational attainment and social inequality, in particular, suggests the importance of both understanding and attacking the problem of low college completion directly. And while college completion is influenced by a wide range of factors, including student and family characteristics, academic preparation, and the cost of college attendance, previous research also suggests that degree completion varies depending on which college students attend.[7] In addition, previous research, including our own, strongly suggests that college enrollment and college choice are strongly influenced by high schools.[8] Given this influence, understanding the ways in which high schools affect students' college going is a logical starting point for thinking about how youth advocates might begin the work of improving college access and attainment among urban youth.

High school effects on college going

Researchers have explored the organizational characteristics of high schools primarily in two broad ways. First, a great deal of research has focused on interpretations of the role of high school guidance counselors. Throughout much of the 1960s and 1970s, a series of sociological studies focused on the role of counselors as "social selectors" or gatekeepers, sorting and screening out students they deemed unfit or unworthy for college.[9] However, over the last four decades, as Rosenbaum and others argue, a combination of greater public awareness of counselors' work, the expansion of community college options, and the advent of open admissions policies have removed much of the impetus for that gatekeeping role, though much of that earlier gatekeeping practice has been replaced with a new kind of "cooling out"—avoidant, often vague, and even misleading college counseling, often failing to provide concrete guidance.[10]

While these richly detailed portraits show how microlevel interactions, strategies, and practices may be key drivers of college-going trends, they may miss the larger ways in which the beliefs, norms, and expectations of the school—frequently grouped together under the banner of school culture and climate—can structure and define the experiences of students as they move through a high school. Schneider has suggested that the efficacy of high schools' direct efforts to support students' college aspirations is determined in large measure by the degree to which those supports are embedded in a network of trusting social relationships among educators, students, and families.[11] A high school with a strong college-going culture, the logic runs, combines both strong academic preparation for college with a powerful set of norms and expectations that arise from educators' shared goals and recognition of their responsibility in helping students achieve them.[12]

Capacity building research

In many ways, these two approaches to thinking about high school effects on college going are complimentary. Viewing the problem of low college attainment from the perspective of high school guidance counselors can provide important insight into how to organize and carry out the work of helping students and their families make the transition to college. By contrast, viewing the problem through the lens of high school culture emphasizes a broader set of issues around how to create and maintain effective systems and structures that will support both the networks of adult relationships and the connections between educators and young people that a college-going culture requires. Analytically, each approach emphasizes different elements of the question; however, outside the context of research, the two approaches also suggest broadly different strategies for not only producing findings but also having an impact.

Over the more than two decades since its founding, CCSR's approach to conducting research has evolved gradually to emphasize a particular kind of partnership between researchers, district officials, and practitioners. In contrast to some of the more traditional roles played by academic researchers in public education—generating big ideas (for example, markets and choice, accountability, and high stakes testing), developing and identifying effective practice models, conducting external program evaluations, and performing traditional policy analyses—CCSR has focused its research around a commitment to building the capacity of practitioners and district officials to think critically about big problems and use data to inform strategic decision-making and evaluation progress.[13] This commitment is organized around three key themes: first, research must remain attached over time to the core problems facing practitioners and district officials; second, researchers must attend carefully to both how adults learn new information and connect it to their work; and finally, researchers must shift from the role of outside expert to interactive participant in building knowledge and searching for solutions.[14]

CCSR's mission to conduct high-quality research that builds the capacity of practitioners and district officials is broadly organized around five critical commitments. Over the last decade, CCSR's postsecondary research group, the Chicago Postsecondary Transition Project, has organized and aligned its work closely with these five commitments: first, developing an extensive data archive on CPS; second, building extensive stakeholder engagement and strong ongoing relationships with CPS; third, conducting scientifically rigorous research while making findings broadly accessible; fourth, building knowledge of core problems across time and across studies; and finally, conducting an extensive outreach to provide information to not only practitioners and district officials, but the broader public as well. As the following sections illustrate, the impact of the research findings has grown to include the development and support of a series of practitioner-driven initiatives to apply that research, to effectively test its implications, and to reveal its limitations and identify future directions. In this chapter, we discuss each of CCSR's five critical commitments in turn, and in each section we provide an illustration of and reflection on that commitment and how it has shaped the progress of the work to improve postsecondary outcomes for young people in CPS.

Developing an extensive data archive on CPS

Building an extensive data archive on CPS is perhaps the most fundamental—and in many ways, one of the most technically challenging—of the five commitments. CCSR researchers depend on the CPS data archive in order to conduct much of the analysis the organization produces; when supplemented with additional data sources, including the CCSR annual student, teacher, and principal surveys, as well as college enrollment and graduation data from the National Student Clearinghouse (NSC), the data archive becomes a powerful resource that allows CCSR researchers to conduct a wide range of studies, remain responsive to district needs, and build knowledge coherently over time and across studies.[15]

The task of developing Chicago's postsecondary tracking system, which began in 2004, illustrates many of the fundamental challenges of creating and maintaining an extensive data archive. Prior to the development of the postsecondary tracking system, most high schools had little or no way to systematically track or analyze their graduates' postsecondary outcomes. In some high schools, staff relied on graduating students' reports about their college plans for the fall; in many high schools, however, staff operated with little or no information whatsoever about their students after graduation. Apart from the goal of conducting research projects, when the postsecondary tracking system was constructed in 2004, there was first and foremost a clear need for accurate, reliable data that the district and schools could use to measure student outcomes, begin to understand college enrollment patters, and then to monitor high schools' efforts to improve.

Linking CPS graduates' academic records with externally verified data on college enrollment from the NSC allowed researchers to confirm students' postsecondary outcomes and to begin to associate them with a host of CCSR student, teacher, and principal survey data and U.S. census data. The creation of a broad, comprehensive data archive including postsecondary outcomes enabled the development of a shared understanding about the importance of school organization and classroom context in educational reform and provided important contextual information about students' home and school communities. This rich, ongoing dataset has allowed researchers to delve deeply into important research questions on the transition to college, leading to the production of a series of pathbreaking reports on college enrollment in the district, the development of the college *match* concept, and a closer look at college readiness in Chicago. However, the more compelling evidence of the postsecondary tracking system's effectiveness as a tool for school reform is visible in district efforts to maintain and expand the system to provide increasingly accurate and more useful information to educators at the high school level.

The district has continued to expand the tracking system over the last decade in response to a growing body of CCSR research pointing up the importance of college choice, college selectivity, and college match. In 2010, the district began not only tracking a college match variable as an individual student outcome but also systematically identifying high-achieving students eligible to attend selective and very selective colleges, using CCSR researcher's criteria for determining students' college access, based on grades, test scores, and advanced coursetaking. The expanded data tracking, in turn, not only allowed the district to target particular students for appropriate programs, interventions, and opportunities, but it also provided critical information to high school counselors and staff members. High schools began receiving lists from central office of their juniors and seniors, sorted according to students' level of college access, in addition to suggestions about which colleges "matched" that level of selectivity. This allowed counselors to organize the work of college counseling and college application in a completely different way, developing different programs, policies, and structures of support for the students with the academic credentials to attend selective colleges than for students with access only to the two-year college system.

Extensive stakeholder engagement and strong ongoing relationships with the district

In addition to the work of creating and maintaining the CPS data archive, CCSR researchers have consistently worked to preserve a deep, collaborative partnership with both the district central office and with practitioners in schools across the city. This is the second critical commitment—to creating extensive stakeholder engagement and strong ongoing relationships with the district. Building engagement and sustaining relationships are both ongoing challenges. Media coverage of CCSR research findings may highlight bad news (for example, high dropout rates, low college enrollment, stagnant test scores, and disorganized school communities) more often than good; however, building trusting, collaborative relationships with not only central office administrators but also with principals, counselors, and teachers across the city is key to creating meaningful, sustained engagement with the difficult questions or problems that the frequently incomplete research provides. One concrete strategy CCSR researchers use to keep the commitment to extensive engagement and ongoing relationships at the center of research efforts is an internal policy to share preliminary research findings as they are being developed before final reports are produced. Sharing findings in their earliest stages is often difficult for researchers to do, but provides district officials and school-based practitioners the opportunity to consider the implications of findings and begin developing policy responses and practice solutions before reports are released.

The CCSR finding that many qualified CPS students were failing to properly file a FAFSA, thereby preventing them from enrolling in college, provides a key illustration of how this approach to ongoing dialog surrounding preliminary findings has worked to build engagement and deepen relationships with district officials and school staff. Beginning in 2006, more than two years before the eventual release of the CCSR report *From High School to the Future: Potholes on the Road to College*, researchers conducting field interviews with a sample of students across three CPS high schools began to realize how confused students were about what FAFSA was, how one filled it out, the differences between filing FAFSA and receiving a PIN for FAFSA, and whether or not applications had officially "gone through." Additional quantitative analysis underscored the finding, showing that among students who were accepted to college, filing a FAFSA was associated with a likelihood of actually enrolling in college twice as high as among those who did not file (see Figure 2.1).

NEW DIRECTIONS FOR YOUTH DEVELOPMENT • DOI: 10.1002.yd

Figure 2.1. Students who were accepted into a four-year college were much more likely to enroll if they completed the FAFSA

Difference in college enrollment by whether students completed their FAFSA among students who were accepted into a four-year college:

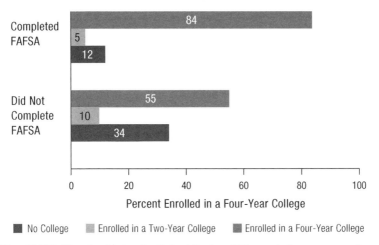

Percent Enrolled in a Four-Year College

■ No College   ■ Enrolled in a Two-Year College   ■ Enrolled in a Four-Year College

Note: FAFSA (Free Application for Federal Student Aid) completion rates come from student responses to the 2005 CPS Senior Exit Questionnaire. Numbers are based on the Potholes Sample (See Appendix B for details).
Source: *Potholes*.

Filing a FAFSA is a time sensitive and, as this analysis indicated, relatively high-stakes proposition for CPS students, many of whom would have seen their college aspirations turn on successfully completing a piece of financial paperwork. CCSR researchers opened a dialog with central office personnel at CPS almost immediately, communicating as much as they knew about FAFSA filing to CPS as quickly as they felt the findings were solid and would not change (even as the analysis around them continued to evolve). At that time, the best practices surrounding college enrollment and financial aid seemed to suggest intensive counseling and support for families near the deadline for filing federal income taxes, in order to cement the link between federal tax returns and FAFSA paperwork. With CCSR's preliminary analysis to partially inform the decision, CPS leadership took a very different approach. Instead of purchasing and implementing an intervention program around financial services, the district built on to its existing postsecondary data tracking system. With the assistance of the Illinois Student Assistance Commission (ISAC), which tracks FAFSA filing in order to administer the Monetary Assistance Program (MAP) grants to Illinois college goers, CPS created a system to generate biweekly, verified reports of all students in the system who had properly filed a FAFSA. At the high school level, these verified FAFSA tracking reports allowed counselors to reorganize a portion of their workload, using these dynamic, accurate lists of students who had not started, had not finished, or had successfully submitted a FAFSA to track and manage this problem. Before CCSR researchers even released the *Potholes* report in 2008, the district had already begun to show progress on one of the most critical findings contained in the report, and the results were dramatic. In 2007, the first year that the district reported FAFSA completion, only 30 percent of seniors had completed a FAFSA by April 1 (a critical deadline for access to many sources of financial aid); by March, 2011, the district reported that the rate had reached 86 percent overall, with a substantial number of schools posting 100 percent completion rates (see Figure 2.2).

Conducting scientifically rigorous research while making findings broadly accessible

CCSR's third critical commitment is to conduct scientifically rigorous research while making the findings from that research broadly accessible to a wide audience. The first CCSR report on college enrollment, *From High School to the Future: A First Look at Chicago Public Schools Graduates' College Enrollment, College Preparation, and Graduation from Four-Year Colleges* in 2006, contributed to a substantial body of existing literature showing that low college access and even lower college attainment among urban students can be attributed in large measure to poor academic preparation for

Figure 2.2. CPS students' college and FAFSA application over time

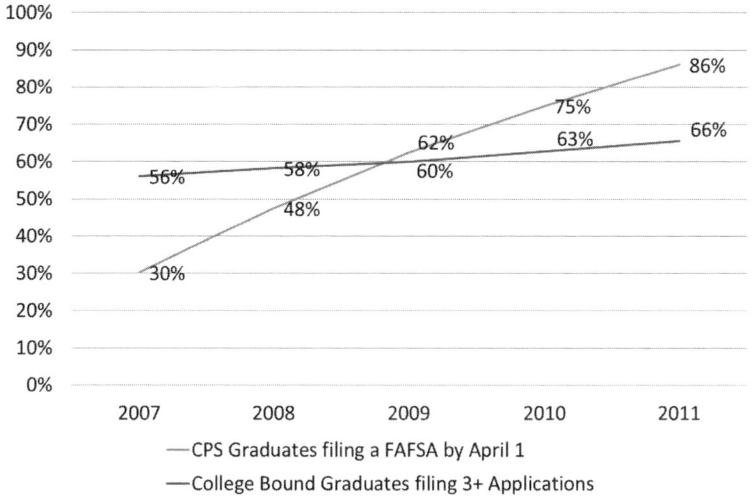

—CPS Graduates filing a FAFSA by April 1
—College Bound Graduates filing 3+ Applications

Source: *CPS Choose Your Future Reports.*

college—low grades, low test scores, and limited participation in advanced coursework. As described above, additional studies also suggested that high schools played an important role in structuring students' access to and decisions about college, both through the individual work of high school counselors and staff members, and through the broader operation of school-level culture and climate surrounding college going. In pushing CCSR's postsecondary research agenda forward, CCSR researchers worked to test these emerging ideas about how high schools might drive college access and enrollment, both to advance the broader research community's understanding of these issues and to inform the work of a local community of policymakers, district officials, and practitioners.

The findings published in the 2008 *Potholes* report on how high schools affected students' college outcomes were not only empirically robust but also analytically fairly complicated. Explaining the analysis derived from rigorously applying hierarchical linear models (HLMs) to understand school effects on students' likelihood of taking steps to search for, apply to, and enroll in four-year

NEW DIRECTIONS FOR YOUTH DEVELOPMENT • DOI: 10.1002.yd

colleges to teachers, counselors, and principals was challenging. Researchers were forced to balance producing a research report using complex, rigorous statistical methods with creating a document that also spoke to policymakers and practitioners in an accessible and compelling way. For this reason, in part, the *Potholes* report made heavy use of a mixed-method approach to research study design, which has become a hallmark of CCSR work over the last two decades. A key finding from *Potholes* was that the most consistent predictor of whether students took the necessary steps toward college enrollment was whether or not they attended a high school with a strong college-going culture, which researchers assessed using a survey measure that asked teachers to report on whether they believed that they and their colleagues at their school expect most students to go to college, help students plan for college, and believe it is their job to prepare students to succeed (see Figure 2.3).

Even controlling for demographic, socioeconomic, and academic characteristics, students who attended high schools that were strong on this measure were significantly more likely to plan to attend college, to apply, to gain acceptance, and to enroll than were similar students in schools with a weak college-going culture. This finding clearly implied that high schools played a critical role in structuring students' opportunities to successfully access postsecondary education, but the people who most needed to understand these findings—teachers, counselors, and school leaders—also needed an entry point for thinking about how to connect this broad finding to their day-to-day work.

The *Potholes* report, as well subsequent reports in the series released in 2009 and 2013, made extensive use of qualitative data, primarily drawing on student interviews and classroom observations, to help practitioners and school leaders think about both the problems raised by the research and the challenge of owning the work of influencing those problems within their schools. In addition to the ongoing quantitative analysis, CCSR researchers completed a longitudinal qualitative study of the high school and postsecondary experiences of a cohort of 105 CPS graduates from three high schools. Following students beginning in their ju-

Figure 2.3. The most consistent school predictor of taking steps toward college enrollment—especially for students with lower academic qualifications—was whether their teachers reported that their school had a strong college climate

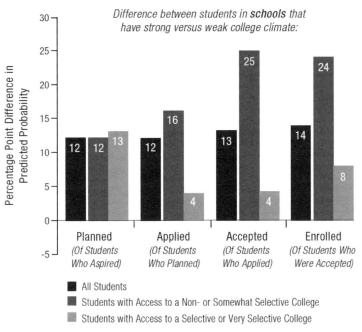

Note: A school with a strong college climate is defined as being 1 standard deviation above the mean and a weak school is 1 standard deviation below the mean. The analysis uses the Potholes Analytic Sample (see Appendix B for details) and adjusts for student demographic, socioeconomic, and academic characteristics. Students are only included in the analysis for a given step if they completed the previous step. See Appendix E for a description of the model used in this anaysis.
Source: *Potholes.*

nior year of high school and continuing into their second year postgraduation, researchers conducted extensive student interviews to better understand postsecondary aspirations, plans, and experiences. The interviews of ten of these students, each representative of a particular pattern of behavior and outcomes from across the sample of students interviewed, became the case studies included in *Potholes*. In many ways, these case studies formed the backbone of the report, connecting findings directly to individual students, many of whom struck practitioners as reflections of the youth they worked with in schools every day. The accessibility of these findings strengthened the report's broader claim that CPS students needed stronger guidance in accessing college, which in turn became a kind of call to action for high schools across the city.

Viewing low college enrollment—and ultimately, low college completion—as at least partially a function of high schools rather than of the students, families, or communities served by CPS represents a major shift in thinking across Chicago and nationally. In the five years since the release of the *Potholes* report, college enrollment rates across CPS have begun to rise. Since the district first reported college enrollment rates in 2006, the proportion of CPS graduates who enroll in college has risen from 48 percent to 60 percent in 2011, and this trend holds across all subgroups of students. The assumption that low rates of college enrollment reflect low student interest in postsecondary education has been effectively discredited across the district. Male students' college enrollment has risen from 45 percent to 55 percent; Latino students from 39 percent to 53 percent; students with ACT scores 17 or below from 38 percent to 48 percent. Similarly, indicators of effective participation in the college planning process, also tracked by the district, have risen. The proportion of college aspirants who completed three or more college applications rose from 56 percent in 2007 to 66 percent in 2011, and students' FAFSA completion increased dramatically (see Figure 2.4).

Building knowledge of core problems across time and across studies

The academic research cycle moves slowly, too often so slowly that research becomes an ineffective tool for driving or supporting ongoing school improvement. The fourth of CCSR's critical commitments is to building knowledge of core problems across time and across studies. Building knowledge for use in the field is a frequently cited goal of academic research; however, developing

Figure 2.4. CPS students' college enrollment over time

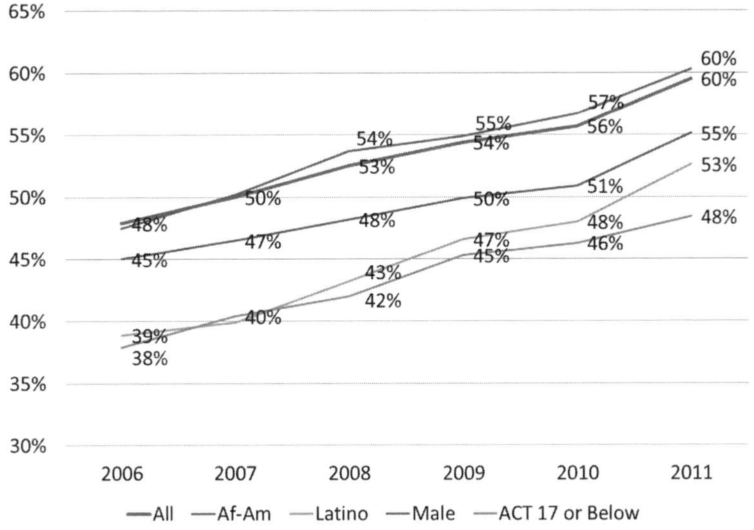

Source: CPS Choose Your Future Reports.

that knowledge over time requires a complicated balance between releasing important findings quickly enough to have an impact on a time-sensitive issue (for example, college enrollment) and building deep, high-quality research that contains both adequate nuance and complexity to make it accurate and compelling. In addition, there is a short window of opportunity for many research findings—the attention of the public or of practitioners may only briefly be trained on an issue, and yet it may take years of sustained engagement with a problem to see results.[16] The release of research findings, in this sense, cannot be a final statement on a problem; rather, it must be an initial stage in a much more durable, sustained process of communicating information. Practically, the commitment to building knowledge of core problems over time and across studies often means releasing findings piecemeal rather than aiming to produce all the findings at the end of a project, as well as working with practitioners on an on-going basis to support their search for solutions in real time. Striking the balance between timeliness and quality, on the one hand, and urgency and sustained engagement on the other hand, is a challenge. However, doing so successfully produces not only more accurate but also more actionable information for practitioners, while also creating an ongoing dialog between researchers and practitioners that further improves the quality and utility of the research itself over time.

In 2006, CCSR researchers produced the first research report in the *From High School to the Future* series, focusing on the college enrollment and graduation patterns of CPS graduates. Although the primary goal of the report was to provide baseline data on CPS students' college enrollment and completion rates, releasing that information without yet answering some critical questions raised by the trends was difficult. For instance, it appeared as though similar high schools serving similar student populations produced very different college enrollment results; how could this be? Perhaps most troubling was the apparent finding that Latino students were far less likely than their peers to enroll in college, even when controlling for student characteristics, high school choice, and academic achievement in high school. Researchers were not able to provide an explanation for this finding in the first report, although it was clear even in 2006 that the rising proportion of Latino students enrolled in CPS schools would only making the issue more pressing over time.

Two years later, in 2008, with the release of the *Potholes* report, researchers were finally able to give schools real insight into college enrollment, casting it ultimately as the result of an underlying gap in students' access to social capital. In the interim, however, a robust conversation about how best to help all students capitalize on their postsecondary aspirations had already begun. Much like the first report in 2006 had, the 2008 release of the *Potholes* report also raised significant unanswered questions about the success of the district's highest-achieving students, which were subsequently addressed in the 2009 follow-up report *From High School to the Future: Making Hard Work Pay Off.* The *Hard Work* report highlighted important and positive trends among students in Chicago's neighborhood International Baccalaureate (IB) programs that were further explored three years later in a working paper on the IB program itself. The repeated advances in researchers' understanding of the nature of college enrollment and completion over this period were matched by a series of methodological innovations along the way, both of which ultimately informed the 2013 report *From High School to the Future: The Challenge of Senior Year in Chicago Public Schools*, which investigated the direct effects of advanced coursetaking on college enrollment and graduation. At each step along the way, researchers released research findings that were incomplete and only partially explained, with the expectation that the information would be both immediately useful to district officials and practitioners and could form the basis for an ongoing mutual engagement in both deepening that understanding and expanding that utility.

An extensive outreach to provide information to broader audiences

The work of understanding and influencing college access and educational attainment in CPS has been a long, complicated, and frequently nonlinear process. Many of the most important ideas—both researchers' and practitioners'—have been, as CCSR cofounder and Carnegie Foundation for Teaching and Learning President Tony Bryk is fond of saying, "possibly wrong and definitely incomplete." However, the evidence of improvement is undeniable and important. Since 2006, in every year, more students have applied to college; larger proportions of students have completed FAFSAs; and greater proportions of students from across all major subgroups have enrolled in college. It is important to recognize, however, that not all of the data are positive, and not all of the problems of college enrollment and especially college completion appear to be solvable with effective data supports and strong school-based case management. Both the successes and the ongoing challenges of this work underscore the importance of the fifth

NEW DIRECTIONS FOR YOUTH DEVELOPMENT • DOI: 10.1002.yd

and final critical commitment to conducting an extensive outreach to provide information to broader audiences. One of the most persistent difficulties of conducting capacity research lies in thinking about the implications of findings—and more specifically, the question of how the findings themselves work their way into how policymakers and practitioners think about a problem, how they view their work, and ultimately, how they approach their daily tasks.

Case study: The college counselors collaborative

One of the primary points of connection between the postsecondary research team and practitioners on the ground has been through the work of the Network for College Success (NCS), a partnership between the University of Chicago School of Social Service Administration and the Chicago Public Schools. The NCS, founded in 2006 by Professor Melissa Roderick, is a network of a dozen CPS high schools that work together to transform high school communities through collaboration, shared learning, and use of data to support postsecondary success for all students. NCS brings research-based, integrated and intensive support for school improvement to principals, their instructional leadership teams, grade level teams, and counselors. The College Counselors' Collaborative (CCC) is one of the core communities of practice within NCS and aims to bring CPS counselors across high schools together in a professional learning community to collaboratively tackle the most challenging problems of practice around postsecondary access and attainment.

Within the CCC, counselors meet monthly, receive job-embedded coaching for the department leader, and have regular access to researchers, who share ongoing research results and also help counselors think about the postsecondary data they have at their disposal. From its inception, one of the primary goals of the CCC was to work on college match, to build their collective knowledge about college options for high-achieving students, to collaboratively build and share best practices for supporting these students' college applications and college choices, and to fastidiously monitor the efficacy of their interventions. From the beginning of this work, it was clear that college match would be harder to influence than FAFSA completion. First, counselors struggled with what metric, exactly, they were trying to move. They knew they wanted to send more of their high-achieving students to colleges that would give them a high probability of degree attainment, but the concept of college match is complex, and, in CCSR research, has always been presented as more of a proxy for high-quality colleges than a causal indicator. Were counselors supposed to aim to enroll students in exact match colleges or in any kind of more selective colleges? Did match mean private colleges? Colleges with higher graduation rates? Smaller colleges? Liberal arts colleges? While the target may have appeared clear (higher match rate), the mechanism for reaching it was anything but.

As the idea of high-quality colleges for high-achieving students continued to evolve, so too did the process of channeling those students toward those options. The first step, made possible by the tracking system, was to have a good understanding of which students in a school's graduating class had access to selective colleges and needed extra support to get there. The support came primarily in the form of help in selecting colleges to apply to and in completing high-quality applications. Counselors in the CCC built their own systems for tracking students' college applications, ensuring that targeted students' choice sets included selective institutions, and also focused on essay writing workshops, help in filling out the common application, and knowledge building among students and the broader school community about graduation rates and financial aid packages at selective schools. The CCC also built an intentional set of relationships with admissions representatives in the Associated Colleges of the Midwest (ACM), a group of small liberal arts colleges. These representatives would have had a hard time justifying the time spent recruiting students from any one of these high schools, who individually serve only a small number of students with access to selective colleges, but since the high schools were organized into a network and able to target the group of students eligible to attend these schools, colleges were much more willing to get involved. The theory of action, the counselors believed, was that if they could get students to change the colleges that they applied to, and if they gained admission to those schools and the schools came through with the financial aid that it appeared was available to this high-need population, students would then choose better colleges.

The result of these efforts was a drastic change in students' application activity. Across about a dozen high schools in the network, applications to ACM colleges rose from virtually zero to over seven hundred in the first full year of program implementation. Acceptances rose as well. In the end, however, the change in students' enrollment was only incremental: matriculation to these schools rose from only a handful of students over the previous five years to about thirty in the first full year of the program. In the broader sense, college match also increased during this time: in these high schools, the proportion of high-achieving students enrolling in selective or very selective colleges rose from 36 percent to 41 percent. It was hard to place these results in context. On the one hand, it was a positive trend where the district remained flat. On the other hand, thirty students did not seem like a lot, given the hundreds of eligible students that were now applying, and the college match increase was not nearly as large as counselors were hoping for. Counselors were sure they could do better but stumped about strategy. As the program continues to evolve, it has become clear that while the strategy of making the college application point a major focal point for counselors' work was enough to change the enrollment patterns of some students, others would need more help.

Conclusion

The five critical commitments discussed and illustrated in this chapter are organized around three broad themes enumerated

NEW DIRECTIONS FOR YOUTH DEVELOPMENT • DOI: 10.1002.yd

above: research must remain connected to the core problems of practice; researchers must focus on and think about how adults learn and use new information in their work; and finally, researchers must be more than outside experts. Since its inception, the work of the postsecondary research group at CCSR has consistently worked within these precepts; the result has been a deep and ongoing partnership between CPS and CCSR in understanding and improving postsecondary outcomes and the forces that shape them. The partnership between CCSR researchers, district officials, and school personnel has already begun to unearth the next set of problems that need to be understood and addressed in order to extend the progress being made.

The challenges of doing this work, including the constant pressure of fundraising to support research, the high-stakes political environment of leadership within large public institutions, and the persistent challenges of poverty low social capital within urban communities, remain. However, the model of capacity-building research outlined and illustrated here suggests that the combination of rigorous research, intentional communication strategies, and ongoing, honest collaboration between researchers and communities of practice is an important model for not only public education but also for youth development more broadly. Building these kinds of intentional partnerships across the youth development field is a complex proposition; however, where these partnerships succeed, we argue, research is not seen as external to the efforts of practitioners to improve the lives of young people, and the efforts of practitioners are not viewed as ancillary to the priorities of professional researchers and the academe.

Notes

1. Goldin, C., & Katz, L. (2008). *The race between education and technology.* Cambridge, MA: Belknap Press of Harvard University Press.

2. Carnevale, A. P., & Rose, S. J. (2010). *The undereducated American.* Washington, DC: Georgetown University, Center on Education and the Workforce; Carnevale, A. P., Strohl, J., & Smith, N. (2009). Help wanted: Postsecondary education and training required. *New Directions for Community Colleges, 146,* 21–31.

3. Roderick, M., Coca, V., Moeller, E., & Kelley-Kemple, T. (2013). *From high school to the future: The challenge of senior year in the Chicago Public Schools.* Chicago, IL: Consortium on Chicago School Research.
4. Bowen, W., Chingos, M., & McPherson, M. (2009). *Crossing the finish line: Completing college at America's public universities.* Princeton, NJ: Princeton University Press.
5. Bowen et al. (2009).
6. Bound, J., Lovenheim, M., & Turner, S. (2007). *Understanding the decrease in college completion rates and the increased time to the baccalaureate degree.* Ann Arbor, MI: Population Studies Center, University of Michigan Institute for Social Research; DesJardins, S. L., Ahlburg, D.A., & McCall, B. P. (2002). Simulating the longitudinal effects of changes in financial aid on student departure from college. *Journal of Human Resources, 37*(3), 653–679; Flores-Lagunes, A., & Light, A. (2010). Interpreting degree effects in the returns to education. *Journal of Human Resources, 45*(2), 439–467; Bound, J., Lovenheim, M. F., & Turner, S. (2012). Increasing time to baccalaureate degree in the United States. *Education Finance and Policy, 7*(4), 375–424.
7. An, B. P. (2010). The relations between race, family characteristics, and where students apply to college. *Social Science Research, 39*(2), 310–323; Coleman, J., Hoffer, T., & Kilgore, S. (1982). *High school achievement: Public, Catholic, and private schools compared.* New York, NY: Basic Books; Falsey, B. & Heyns, B. (1984). The college channel: Private and public schools reconsidered. *Sociology of Education, 57,* 111–122; Hurtado, S., Inkelas, K. K., Briggs, C., & Rhee, B. S. (1997). Differences in college access and choice among racial/ethnic groups: Identifying continuing barriers. *Research in Higher Education, 38*(1), 43–75; Meyer, J. (1970). High school effects on college intentions. *American Journal of Sociology, 76*(1), 59–70; Perna, L. W., & Titus, M. A. (2005). The relationship between parental involvement as social capital and college enrollment: An examination of racial/ethnic group differences. *Journal of Higher Education, 76*(5), 485–518; Adelman, C. (2006). *The toolbox revisited: Paths to degree completion from high school through college.* Washington, DC: U.S. Department of Education; Pike, G. R., & Saupe, J. L. (2002). Does high school matter? An analysis of three methods of predicting first-year grades. *Research in Higher Education, 43*(2), 187–207; Dynarski, S. M. (1999). *Does aid matter? Measuring the effect of student aid on college attendance and completion* (NBER Working Paper No. 7422). Cambridge, MA: National Bureau of Economic Research; John, E. P. S., Paulsen, M. B., & Starkey, J. B. (1996). The nexus between college choice and persistence. *Research in Higher Education, 37*(2), 175–220; Kane, T. 1999. The price of admission: Rethinking how Americans pay for college. Washington, DC: Brookings Institution Press; Velez, W. (1985). Finishing college: The effects of college type. *Sociology of Education, 58*(3), 191–200; McDonough, P. (1997). *Choosing colleges: How social class and schools structure opportunity.* Albany, NY: State University of New York Press.
8. Roderick, M., Nagaoka, J., Coca, V., & Moeller, E. (2008). *From high school to the future: Potholes on the road to college.* Chicago, IL: Consortium on Chicago School Research; Engberg, M. E., & Wolniak, G. C. (2010).

Examining the effects of high school contexts on postsecondary enrollment. *Research in Higher Education*, *51*(2), 132–153; Nuñez, A. M., & Kim, D. (2012). Building a multicontextual model of Latino college enrollment: Student, school, and state-level effects. *The Review of Higher Education*, *35*(2), 237–263; Wolniak, G. C., & Engberg, M. E. (2007). The effects of high school feeder networks on college enrollment. *The Review of Higher Education*, *31*(1), 27–53; Hill, L. (2008). School strategies and the "college-linking" process: Reconsidering the effects of high schools on college enrollment. *Sociology of Education*, 81, 53–76.

    9. Rosenbaum, J., Miller, S. R., & Krei, M. S. (1996). Gatekeeping in an era of more open gates: High school counselors' views of their influence on students' college plans. *American Journal of Education*, *104*(4), 257–279; Cicourel, A. V., & Kitsuse, J. I. (1963). *The educational decision makers: An advanced study in sociology*. Indianapolis, IN: Bobbs-Merrill; Schafer, W. E., & Olexa, C. (1971). *Tracking and opportunity*. Scranton, PA: Chandler; Rosenbaum, J. (1976). *Making inequality*. New York, NY: Wiley; Erickson, F. (1975). Gatekeeping and the melting pot: Interaction in counseling encounters. *Harvard Educational Review*, *45*(1), 44–70; Heyns, B. (1974). Social selection and stratification within schools. *American Journal of Sociology*, *79*(6), 1434–1451.

    10. Rosenbaum et al. (1996).

    11. Schneider, B. (2007). *Forming a college-going community in US public high schools*. New Delhi, India: Bill & Melinda Gates Foundation.

    12. Schneider. (2007).

    13. Roderick, M., Easton, J., & Bender Sebring, P. (2009). *A new model for the role of research in supporting urban school reform*. Chicago, IL: Consortium on Chicago School Research.

    14. Roderick et al. (2009).

    15. Roderick et al. (2009).

    16. Roderick et al. (2009).

DAVID W. JOHNSON *is the associate director for postsecondary studies at the University of Chicago Consortium on Chicago School Research.*

ELIZA MOELLER *is a research analyst at the University of Chicago Consortium on Chicago School Research.*

MATHEW HOLSAPPLE *is a research analyst at the University of Chicago Consortium on Chicago School Research.*

This chapter discusses the collaboration between a national college access program, the National College Advising Corps, and its research and evaluation team at Stanford University. In an effort to benefit other programs seeking to form successful data-driven interventions, we provide explicit examples of the partnership and present several examples of how the program has benefited from the data gathered by the evaluation team.

3

Lessons learned from a data-driven college access program: The National College Advising Corps

*Eileen L. Horng, Brent J. Evans,
anthony l. antonio, Jesse D. Foster,
Hoori S. Kalamkarian,
Nicole F. Hurd, Eric P. Bettinger*

PROMOTING COLLEGE ACCESS and student success is an important policy goal to maintain an effective society and competitive economy. Too many academically able students are not enrolling in postsecondary education, and that comes at a cost of millions of unattained bachelor's degrees across the nation.[1] One of the documented causes of this problem is that many students do not have

Each author contributed equally, and we determined author order randomly. Nicole Hurd is the executive director of the National College Advising Corps and contributed to the section on how NCAC uses evaluation data to drive program reform. The remainder of the authors make up the Stanford evaluation and research team.

the necessary information and support to navigate the complex college search, application, and selection processes. The college application process itself requires completing a complicated series of procedures that many students find bewildering.[2] Furthermore, the financial aid application process has been described as a gauntlet presenting imposing barriers that many students struggle to overcome.[3]

One of the major responses to this complexity has been the development of college access programs and interventions. These efforts work directly with students and their families to overcome the information and complexity obstacles to applying to and entering college. Although evaluations of these programs have produced varied results, recent and ongoing work suggests that helping students navigate these processes improve their educational outcomes. For instance, Bettinger, Long, Oreopoulos, and Sanbanmatsu demonstrate that providing assistance in completing the federal financial aid application improves college enrollment.[4]

The National College Advising Corps (NCAC) is one such college access and success program currently active in nearly four hundred high schools across fourteen different states. The program's goal is twofold. First, it provides necessary information and support for students who may find it difficult to navigate the complex college admission process. Second, the advisers conduct outreach to underclassmen in an effort to improve the school-wide college-going culture.

The program partners institutions of higher education with underserved high schools to provide a recent college graduate as a full-time college adviser. The advisers work with high school students on a variety of college preparatory activities, such as the college search process, the application process, test preparation and registration, and financial aid applications. The program is a full school model in which the advisers work with any student who requests assistance as opposed to a cohort-based model in which the adviser only works with a subset of students from the school.

This chapter discusses our research team's multiyear collaboration with the National College Advising Corps. This collaboration

NEW DIRECTIONS FOR YOUTH DEVELOPMENT • DOI: 10.1002.yd

has successfully combined evaluating the program's effectiveness with scholarly research that will contribute to the broader literature on college access. These studies will be helpful for both policymakers and practitioners as we move toward a more complete understanding of how best to support high school students making the transition to postsecondary education.

The chapter is structured as follows. We first describe the various data sources we compile and consider when evaluating how successful the program is at improving college enrollment and instilling a college-going culture in high schools. Then we turn to discuss the established partnerships between the evaluation and research team, national office, state program directors, and local schools. We also present summaries of the current research projects under study in coordination with the program evaluation. Finally, we describe how NCAC uses the data and findings from the research and evaluation team to improve their program.

Triangulation of data sources

As we began collaborating to design an evaluation, we had to weigh the diverse interests of stakeholders and the diverse understanding among stakeholders of different types of evidence. For example, many of NCAC's funders wanted to see qualitative data in the form of anecdotes. In contrast, other funders wanted quantitative, even causal, evidence. Different stakeholders had different levels of trust and comfort with different methods and sources of evidence. Some stakeholders did not trust the black box of quantitative analysis while others worried about the representativeness of qualitative data.

Our goal was that each stakeholder would learn from the evaluation. To make this happen, we elected to conduct the evaluation in multiple parts. First, we divided our team into three parts—one which would gather data through qualitative methods, particularly using interviews and observations conducted during site visits of selected schools; another which would focus on surveys of advisers and students; and yet another which would focus on administrative data on subsequent college attendance (for example, data from the National Student Clearinghouse). Each team used either or both qualitative and quantitative methods depending on the data source. Once each team was formed, we then proceeded with the data collection aiming to triangulate the evaluation and to analyze the key research questions with different methods and data. While the teams shared data to facilitate triangulation of evaluation findings and the development of research-focused inquiries, each team aimed to provide a unique perspective based on the data they had available.

By relying on both quantitative and qualitative social science tools, we were able to examine the many facets of the program and to provide both descriptive and causal evidence. Survey data from high school students provide an account of participants' college knowledge and preparation and how these may have changed through interactions with the NCAC adviser. Survey data from NCAC advisers allow us to examine the interactions advisers have in their schools with colleagues and students and to explore the impact of participation in NCAC on their own lives. Site visit data afford a rich understanding of the role the advisers play in their schools and the impact they have on their schools' college-going cultures. Data on subsequent college enrollment provide evidence on changes in long-run outcomes. The combination of these multiple sources of data provides this evaluation with breadth and depth.

Student survey data

The student survey gives NCAC an opportunity to track student decisions with respect to college preparation activities at partner high schools. We rely on these data to identify the specific steps that students have taken to prepare for college. The survey also provides insights into students' preparation for college and motivation to continue their education. The student survey also allows NCAC to identify potential levers where advisers can increase their efficacy.

NEW DIRECTIONS FOR YOUTH DEVELOPMENT • DOI: 10.1002.yd

The survey focuses on four types of questions: (1) demographic information, including grade, parental education, ethnicity, and gender; (2) postsecondary aspirations; (3) college preparation activities; and (4) college knowledge. The first category captures socioeconomic and demographic factors associated with differential college aspirations, preparation, and admission outcomes. The second category includes measures of the resultant influence of all contexts on students' outlooks on college. The third are indicators of behaviors along the pathway related to college going, and the fourth measures specific knowledge emanating from the federal policy context.

The survey primarily targets seniors who are making college decisions. Students are surveyed annually in April and May, when they are far enough along in the planning process that they likely have a clear idea of whether and where they will attend college in the coming year. In addition to asking students about their college plans, we ask them to reflect on their academic preparation throughout high school. We also ask them about what college-going information they received and from whom they received it. The student survey data help us to identify important trends in NCAC schools. We rely on these data to identify the specific steps that students have taken to prepare for college.

Most recently, we invited 168 schools to participate in the student survey across nine states, and we achieved a 67 percent student response rate among these schools.

Adviser survey

Every spring, we also ask current NCAC advisers to complete a survey. The survey gathers data on the full spectrum of college advising efforts at the school as well as to understand advisers' thoughts on the program. The survey asks advisers to discuss some of the experiences that they have with students, teachers, parents, and administrators. The survey questions cover a broad array of topics, such as the level of coordination on college access efforts at the school, how advisers spend their time, and what their future study and career prospects are. The 2012 adviser survey was conducted online in May. It is important to note that the timing captured advisers at the end of the school year after the majority of college application and FAFSA filings have taken place. By this time in the school year, even the first-year advisers have a thorough understanding of their students and of the operation of their school(s). In 2012, every adviser completed the survey.

National Student Clearinghouse data

NCAC collects lists of graduating seniors from partner high schools. We submit these lists for matching with the National Student Clearinghouse (NSC) on behalf of NCAC. The NSC provides FERPA-compliant access to a nationwide coverage of postsecondary enrollment and degree records. Over 3,300 colleges and universities, enrolling over 93 percent of all students in public and private U.S. institutions, participate in the Clearinghouse. Using NSC, we have tracked the collegiate experiences of 260,412 students from over 150 high schools across eight states.

Site visits

The purpose of the site visits is to examine how NCAC is being experienced by various actors in the schools, and in particular, what type of impact they report the program is having on the college-going culture of its schools. This qualitative approach allows us to provide a more holistic and in-depth description of program operations and functioning within schools. The primary mission of NCAC is to raise the rates of college enrollment and completion among low-income, first-generation college students, but the process by which this mission is carried out varies significantly by individual, by type of stakeholder, and by school. It is this microlevel, operational aspect of the program that is important to understand if it is to have an impact on college-going culture. Specifically, in what way is the program disrupting, complementing, or enhancing the college-preparation behavior, activities, and attitudes of the different stakeholders?

In spring 2011, we conducted seventeen site visits in five states and interviewed the primary stakeholders implicated in the college

NEW DIRECTIONS FOR YOUTH DEVELOPMENT • DOI: 10.1002.yd

advising efforts at each school, specifically, administrators, teachers, counselors, parents, students, NCAC advisers, and any additional college advising personnel (for example, GEAR UP coordinators). In total, we conducted 112 interviews at the seventeen schools. The stakeholders at each school were either interviewed in groups or individually depending on the type of stakeholder and their availability (for example, students and parents tended to be interviewed in groups whereas school staff tended to be interviewed individually). Individual interviews lasted approximately thirty minutes, while group interviews lasted forty-five minutes to an hour. Most interviews were conducted on site at the school, although a handful had to be completed by phone due to time restrictions. All interviews were recorded, transcribed, and coded using Atlas.ti analytic software. We developed the coding scheme using a grounded theory approach, which was developed and validated by a team of three researchers.

Triangulation

As we mentioned, each source of information provides unique data on some aspect of the program. We gather data on advisers through the adviser surveys, student surveys, and interviews. Each gathers similar data on advisers, and we can triangulate the sources to create a concrete picture as to the advisers' strengths and weaknesses. Similarly, we can triangulate evidence on school leadership, teacher participation, parental participation, and student preparation and initiative. With the additional National Student Clearinghouse data, we can triangulate on the program's overall efficacy.

One concrete example of this method relates to how advisers work with teachers. We discovered very early through the student survey that teachers are an important resource for information on college going among high school students. Through the adviser survey we asked how advisers interact with teachers and how smoothly that coordination works. Site visits explored this interaction more deeply in a smaller number of sites, and administrative data from the National Student Clearinghouse enable us to examine whether differences in enrollment rates correlate with teacher and adviser interactions.

Partnerships

Many partnerships are critical to the success of a data-driven educational intervention. Perhaps the most important of these is the partnership between the researchers and the National College Advising Corps. The partnership focuses primarily on the evaluation of program effectiveness with the aim of continuous improvement. This shared objective requires several shared assumptions:

- All evaluation results are welcome. Positive, negative, and inconclusive results are all valuable for understanding the nature of programmatic impact.
- Scholarly research is welcome. A successful intervention is guided by both data-driven programmatic assessment as well as research-focused scholarly inquiry.
- Data are preeminent. All personnel, from research team to individual advisers, need to expend appropriate effort to successfully gather critical data.
- Research and evaluation informs design. The work of the research team is expected to influence programmatic design.
- Programmatic considerations inform design. The realities of implementation, the need to be locally responsive to stakeholders, and the wisdom of engaged practitioners are expected to guide research design.

With these shared assumptions, we aimed to develop a collaboration that would yield both valuable evaluation data as well as research for broader impact in the field. From the outset of our collaboration, research and evaluation considerations were central to programmatic discussions of grant writing, program expansion, and local assessment needs. Integral to this collaboration is built-in communication across research and practice. For example, the research team is routinely invited to monthly programmatic meetings. Additionally, the research team presents developing and completed research projects to NCAC central staff and regional program directors nationwide. The research team also presents research findings and information about the evaluation to the actual advisers once per year. With this structure and key shared assumptions, we strike a continual balance between the programmatic needs of evaluation and our own research objectives in the area of college access.

Several other partnerships are critical to the NCAC program as well as our research and evaluation work. We discuss the most important among them below.

Program design: Federal, regional, and local levels

To administer the advising program, NCAC relies on two types of institutional partnerships. First, NCAC partners with postsecondary institutions willing to host the program by facilitating space and staff as regional program directors. Currently, NCAC partners with eighteen colleges and universities across fourteen states. The organization supports the partnering universities through fundraising, evaluation services, oversight, and an annual training for advisers.

These postsecondary institutions, in turn, partner with local school districts and schools to place NCAC advisers in high-need high schools. In these university-district-school partnerships, the college- or university-based program directors assume the responsibility to recruit and hire the NCAC advisers. In addition to the national training, the directors facilitate multiweek regional trainings during the summer. Moreover, directors regularly monitor advisers' activities. For example, directors require advisers to set quarterly goals, such as meeting with a percentage of the senior class and track their progress toward these goals. As necessary, directors also assume the responsibility to mediate challenges that providers and school staff experiences while working together. For example, at one school in California, the adviser found it challenging to engage with the school principal and garner support for the activities; this adviser relied on the program director to mediate the relationship with the principal and clarify the program's objectives. This adviser described the director's contribution noting:

And so (the program director) would come in and you know, just kinda sit down and say you know, I know you're (the principal) really busy but you know, especially at this moment it's really important for the students to be exposed to this message of college and you know, and it'll help them with their school work. It'll provide an incentive for them to get their school— so she's really good at sorta figuring out what like catering to what they would wanna hear but kind of working in our agenda as well.

While program directors oversee the advising program, high schools hosting an adviser retain some autonomy in shaping the advising program to meet their needs. A staff member, often a guidance counselor, is assigned as the adviser's immediate school-based supervisor. Advisers work with these school-based supervisors to determine the adviser's scope of work at the high school. Given this flexibility, in some schools, counselors use advisers to fully oversee college preparation allowing the counseling department to focus on other forms of advising. In other schools, school-based supervisors more closely coordinate their efforts with the advising program and collaborate with the adviser to codesign and host college-oriented workshops.

The university-district-school partnership design facilitates opportunities for partners to tangentially benefit from the college advising program. Often, the increased attention on postsecondary planning and pathways that advisers contribute aligns with the district's efforts around college and career readiness. As an example, during our site visits, school staff and advisers often noted that in an effort to promote college going, districts were implementing new policies to pay ACT or SAT registration fees for juniors and seniors; the advisers' efforts to meet with upperclassmen and encourage seniors to apply to college further enhanced the impact of these district policies on college going. District and school personnel also often gained more detailed, timely knowledge of the college application process from recently trained advisers. In one case, district personnel and school-based supervisors attended a regional training for advisers hosted by the university-based program director to learn more about recent changes to the college application process.

Our evaluation team also contributes to these multilevel partnerships by providing data at all levels. We rely on the individual advisers' contact logs to record all of the interactions they have with students in each high school. We then aggregate those reports at the state level and provide monthly summaries to the program directors at each partner university. We also aggregate state numbers to provide monthly summaries to the national office. Finally, we provide trend data to program directors and the national office in annual program reports.

Although working with each individual high school requires immense logistical coordination, both the evaluation and the high schools gain from the collaboration. High schools provide lists of graduating students each year that the evaluation team matches to the National Student Clearinghouse. We then produce school-level reports that provide detailed information on the college enrollment patterns of their graduates over several years including charts and tables of two-year and four-year college enrollment rates, full-time enrollment rates, and college persistence rates. Most high schools are unaware of the college enrollment rates of their graduates, and this report provides them with a baseline level of college enrollment so that they can monitor changes to their enrollment rates as time progresses. For some schools, the numbers come as a surprise and highlight that additional emphasis needs to be placed on college preparation. Schools appreciate this individualized level of analysis, and it encourages their continued cooperation with our data collection and evaluation efforts.

Research relationships with individual states

During the first year of the partnership between NCAC and Stanford University, the research and evaluation efforts took an expansive approach. The overarching goal was to understand the wide scale impact of the program across multiple states. As the program matured, establishing long-term relationships within states as well as broaching new territory, it became important to focus our efforts on particular cases. This section provides an overview of two such cases: one a robust data gathering effort on the newest and largest NCAC program in Texas, and the other an in-depth qualitative case study of established NCAC schools in Missouri.

Texas. In the 2010–2011 school year, Texas piloted implementation of the NCAC model in fifteen high schools in the state. The following school year (2011–2012), the statewide NCAC program, known as Advise TX, was expanded to 120 schools in multiple regions across the state, marking an 800 percent growth in the span of a single year. The vast expansion of Advise TX afforded a unique and necessary opportunity to gather robust data on the program's effect on various college outcomes.

Prior to this, evaluations of NCAC's success in schools across several states employed a difference-in-differences methodology to focus on college enrollment outcomes. Difference-in-differences compares trends across treatment and control groups before and after the inception of a new program. In this case, the treatment group includes schools that have an NCAC adviser currently operating on the site. Control schools are high schools in the same or neighboring school districts that do not have an NCAC adviser. Both rural and urban schools were included in the analysis, although the percentage of each varies by state. The study made comparisons across approximately ninety NCAC and non-NCAC schools over the period 2006–2009.

Results vary substantially across states. The variance of these results is driven in part by different numbers of control schools used in the analysis. While some of this evidence points to the efficacy of the NCAC intervention, results are somewhat inconclusive. Because the evidence is mixed, a larger study incorporating experimental methods and a larger number of treatment and control schools was necessary. The sheer size of the Texas program provides an incredible opportunity for such a study. By randomizing which schools receive advisers and tracking college enrollment rates at thirty-six treatment and seventy-six control schools, in future years, our evaluation of Advise TX should provide conclusive evidence of the impact of the program on the college-going rate of high schools.

In addition to the experimental opportunities afforded by the size of the Texas program, we have been able to collect complementary quantitative and qualitative data, including student and adviser surveys; school-level administrative data, such as socioeconomic variables (for example, racial distribution and free/reduced lunch population), academic variables (for example, TAKS scores and graduation rates), and other descriptive variables (for example, size); and finally, daylong site visits to multiple Advise TX schools where interviews with teachers, administrators, counselor, students, and parents were conducted.

The partnership with Advise TX has provided important information on the rapid growth and integration of a young program, particularly in a state where there is no shortage of external providers working closely with schools. By establishing an early and long-term partnership with the NCAC program in a single state, we are able to identify meaningful trends and college-going outcomes affected by NCAC, while trying to understand the context in which these effects arise.

Missouri. Beginning in fall 2012, we focused the qualitative component of the research and evaluation activities on single-state case studies. Throughout the partnership with NCAC, the goal of the qualitative case studies has been to understand the program's impact on the college-going culture of various high schools. Studies on college-going culture demonstrate the positive impact a school can have on students' aspirations and college-going rates.[5] In order to explore variation in cultures in different school environments, it was necessary to collect interview and more in-depth observation data that allow us to explore values, expectations, attitudes, and behaviors related to college going and college preparation across entire schools. With these case studies, it was possible to examine and describe more and less cohesive cultures and identify the existence of fragmented or segmented cultures.

Figure 3.1. Two-by-two matrix design

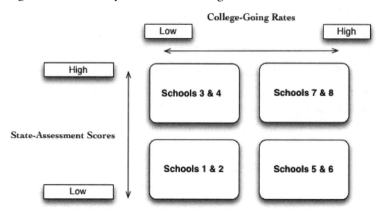

By focusing our efforts on a single state, we were able to de-sign week-long site visits per school. Between the months of September–November of 2012, we visited eight high school campuses across three areas of Missouri. Each of the schools had a well-established relationship with NCAC, such that they had become accustomed to working with a college adviser. The eight schools varied in terms of the length of their relationship with NCAC, but at minimum, they were on their second adviser. The research team used maximum variation sampling to select case schools based upon college-going culture, utilizing college-going rates and state assessment scores as a proxy for college-going culture. A two-by-two matrix design was used to guide this site-selection process. Figure 3.1 provides an overview of the two-by-two design; two schools were selected from each cell for a total of eight possible sites.

Each of the eight schools participated in these extended site visits during which multiple types of interviews and observations were conducted by a two-person research team. In addition to multiple interviews with teachers, administrators, counselors, students (9th–12th grade), and parents, observations were conducted of (1) college-related events (for example, college fairs and campus tours), (2) classroom presentations on college preparation, (3) college advising sessions with individual students, and (4) interaction between the college adviser and other school staff. Inquiry generally focused on how the school was organized to prepare students for postsecondary education, including how attitudes toward college varied among stakeholders, how different staff members discussed and promoted college, and how intrastaff collaboration supported college-going efforts throughout the school.

This in-depth, qualitative approach has allowed us to develop a more complex understanding of college-going culture than currently exists in the literature. Specifically, we have created a typology of college-going culture that allows us to identify where schools fall in their college-going practices and attitudes and also where there are gaps in their approach. That is, which types of students are not being reached and which staff members are absent from college preparation efforts? Moving forward, we will continue to use a single-state case study approach to explore specific cultural features and the means by which an external provider can make a cultural impact.

Scholarly studies

The NCAC evaluation facilitates a unique opportunity for Stanford University research faculty and graduate students to pursue scholarly research while simultaneously meeting evaluation objectives. This section delineates three research projects in varying stages of completion currently under pursuit by members of our team. By combining our array of data sources with qualitative and quantitative analyses, we are able to unite the evaluation and research agendas. These projects both inform practice and deepen our conceptual understanding of the conditions and practices that shape college access.

College-going culture

This research project examines the organization of college advising and the expression of normative college-going culture in schools. Empirical research on college-going cultures is relatively scarce, leaving our understanding of college-going culture in schools as fairly simplistic and undertheorized. In this project, we utilize the rich case study data of eleven high schools and conceptualize a typology of college-going cultures to guide further research as well as continuing culture-building efforts in schools. With our typology, we are able to categorize schools across two conceptual axes. First, we identify schools based on whether their approach to college reflects a more integrative or *cohesive* organizational culture or whether it reflects a differentiated, fragmented or *diffuse* culture. Second, we illustrate that some schools conceptualize and enact college going as being highly central to their overall mission—it is the primary expectation they have for their students. That is, all students are expected to go to college and it is seen as a natural next step. Other schools, which we designate as low-centrality schools present a view of college going that is less central to the overall mission—college is presented as one of several options available to students, and one that is not necessarily for everyone.

Advise Texas experiment

Given the multiple approaches high schools often take to improving college enrollment among their graduates, determining the efficacy of the NCAC program in isolation is a challenge. Thanks to federal funding from a U.S. Department of Education Challenge Grant, Texas increased the number of high schools with an NCAC adviser from 15 to 120 in one academic year. We identified this rapid expansion as a unique opportunity to experimentally study the impact of the program by randomly assigning advisers to high schools. We are currently compiling data on college preparation activities from student surveys and data on college enrollment from the Texas Higher Education Coordinating Board for both treatment and control schools.

College advising dosage experiment

While the Texas experiment randomly assigns advisers at the school level so that we obtain school-wide impact estimates of the adviser's presence, we are also interested in the individual level impact of working with an adviser. To answer this question, the dosage treatment study randomly assigns students within NCAC high schools to receive extra attention and support from the adviser (a higher dosage of the NCAC program). This study randomly assigns this extra focus of effort to thirty students with high school GPAs between 2.0 and 3.0 at the beginning of their senior year in each of about twenty NCAC schools across four states. Preliminary analyses indicate that randomization produced balance across treatment and control, and the treatment group received a higher level of interaction with the advisers than the control group. College enrollment results will indicate whether additional meetings with the adviser are productive.

Data-driven program changes

Because the program integrated an evidence-based approach from the onset, the program's culture is imbued with a data-driven mentality at all levels from the director and oversight board to the individual advisers. We communicate results of the evaluation and research to all of the advisers during a national summer institute, and we believe an awareness of the findings improves their effectiveness. In concert with the developing literature on college access, data obtained from the research and evaluation team inform programmatic practice in numerous ways. We highlight three specific examples: developing key performance indicators (KPIs) and accountability, advising on the growth strategy, and involving teachers and parents in promoting college access.

Our first-year evaluation report contained a wealth of descriptive information that was previously unknown to the national office such as how many college workshops the advisers were hosting. Out of this report, they developed eight KPIs that have driven every aspect of the program including training, implementation, and evaluation. NCAC's initial funders were primarily interested in college enrollment statistics. While these are undoubtedly important, the evaluation provided very clear information on the intermediate steps to achieving increased college enrollment rates, such as visiting a college, registering for the SAT/ACT, submitting a college application, and completing the FAFSA. These measures now serve as the KPIs currently pursued by the advisers. In collaboration with regional program directors, we also developed a student tracker data collection system in which advisers monitor and record their interactions with each student. This individualized level of data collection promotes accountability of each adviser as well as at the partner institution level.

The program expects to move from serving the current number of 389 schools to reaching over 1,000 high schools in the next five years. Data collected for the evaluation facilitate this growth trajectory in several ways. First, we assist in selecting high schools most in need of college advising support using state and district level data. Second, our qualitative research identified the importance of school leadership in promoting a college-going culture, so the program directors are attuned to selecting schools with cooperative principals and guidance staff. Program directors have also disseminated the message of how valuable school leadership can be to improving college access and assisting in the program's success. Third, the program ensures a baseline level of success thanks to the evaluation identifying poor performing schools and programs which can result in corrective action or even program termination at those schools. Finally, we convinced the national office that the quantity of data needed for a robust evaluation requires extensive logistical support that will be provided by a newly created director of measurement and insight position housed in the national office.

One of the most surprising results of the evaluation appeared in the student survey responses. When asked with whom they most often discuss college-going issues, students overwhelmingly report that their teachers and parents are the two most important groups. These findings prompted two changes to the structure of the program. The initial NCAC structure focused on the advisers providing necessary college information directly to students in isolation or in collaboration with the school's guidance office. The revised model incorporates an intentional effort to work with teachers as the advisers' partners in promoting a college-going culture. Advisers now commonly hold information sessions in teachers' classes, and they identify partner teachers that integrate college materials into their normal daily lessons. Our studies also discovered that many students claimed they did not know anyone that had attended college, never realizing that all of their teachers are college graduates. To rectify this situation, advisers in NCAC schools ask teachers to put the name of the college the teacher attended outside their classroom door.

The second change in the program in response to our survey results is an increased effort at parent outreach. Parents are a key component in encouraging college enrollment, and advisers should view them as partners in the effort to increase the number of students' applications to college. The survey results prompted NCAC advisers to host more parent information nights and build relationships with parents in the communities in which they live. One adviser took tickets at high school football games in order to meet as many families of their seniors as possible. Others reach out to community organizations such as churches to disseminate information to parents that are difficult to attract to school.

Conclusion

The philosophy undergirding the collaboration of the NCAC program with our evaluation team is to pursue mutually advantageous goals. The evaluation and research projects enhance the program's effectiveness. In return, the research team is able to use the NCAC program as a laboratory for investigating important questions about college access that can be applied more widely in policy and practice.

One potential concern with this style of ongoing partnership is that negative findings are dismissed or, at worse, hidden. Throughout our work, we have been forthcoming when we obtained negative results, and the national office has welcomed them as opportunities to identify problems and improve the program. This willingness to receive feedback from all evaluation results—"everything, warts and all"—encourages a wider array of useful studies because the evaluation does not need to focus solely on the most promising components of the program.

Being a successful, data-driven program requires three components. First, a mutual understanding of both the program's and evaluators' goals ensures that both sides are benefiting from the partnership. Second, open lines of communication throughout all levels of the organization and with the data analysts ensure that important information learned from the evaluation spread to everyone in the organization who could benefit. Finally, receptiveness to learning from the data and altering the program when results suggest improvements can be made is key to developing a successful intervention.

Notes

1. Advisory Committee on Student Financial Assistance. (2006). *Mortgaging our future*. Washington, DC: Author.

2. Klasik, D. (2012). The college application gauntlet: A systematic analysis of the steps to four-year college enrollment. *Research in Higher Education, 53*, 506–549.

3. Advisory Committee on Student Financial Assistance. (2005). *The student aid gauntlet: Making access to college simple and certain*. Washington, DC: Author.

4. Bettinger, E. P., Long, B. T., Oreopoulos, P., & Sanbonmatsu, L. (2012). The role of application assistance and information in college decisions: Results from the H&R block FAFSA experiment. *Quarterly Journal of Economics, 127*, 1205–1242.

5. McDonough, P. M. (1997). *Choosing colleges: How social class and schools structure opportunity*. Albany, NY: SUNY Press.

EILEEN L. HORNG *is a partner at Evaluation and Assessment Solutions for Education.*

BRENT J. EVANS *is an assistant professor of public policy and higher education in the Peabody College at Vanderbilt University.*

ANTHONY L. ANTONIO *is an associate professor of education at Stanford University.*

JESSE D. FOSTER *is a doctoral candidate at Stanford University.*

HOORI S. KALAMKARIAN *is a doctoral candidate at Stanford University.*

NICOLE F. HURD *is the founder and CEO of the College Advising Corps.*

ERIC P. BETTINGER *is an associate professor in the School of Education at Stanford University.*

Text messaging and peer mentoring programs are shown to be helpful and cost-effective strategies for addressing the phenomenon of "summer melt" observed among low-income college-intending students.

4

The not-so-lazy days of summer: Experimental interventions to increase college entry among low-income high school graduates

Benjamin L. Castleman, Lindsay C. Page

THE SUMMER AFTER high school graduation occupies a treasured place in American culture. Popular movies and music portray high school seniors whiling away the final days of the academic year in dreamy expectation of lazy days on the beach and coming-of-age road trips to unfamiliar destinations. If students feel any anxiety at all, it is brought about by the nervous anticipation of first phone calls (or Facebook chats) with soon-to-be college roommates or by the daunting task of choosing the duvet that best matches the overall dorm room décor.

But does this conception of the post-high school summer accurately capture the experience of low-income, college-intending high school graduates? Scholars have documented the phenomenon of "summer fadeout," where children, especially those from families with low incomes, suffer achievement declines between the end of one school year and the start of the next.[1] Nevertheless, prevailing psychological and sociological theories of college choice and retention neglect to consider the possibility that students may change their postsecondary plans during the summer after high school.[2]

After students have been accepted to and have decided to attend a particular college, however, they must complete a complicated array of tasks in order to successfully matriculate. For instance, students must interpret their financial aid award, identify any financial gap between their aid package and the cost of attendance, and make a plan for how they will acquire the necessary funds to fill this gap. Students also typically need to complete a number of administrative tasks, such as registering for and attending freshman orientation, registering for and completing academic placement tests, and completing housing forms.[3] Such tasks may be particularly onerous for students from disadvantaged backgrounds who are often isolated from professional guidance and support: low-income students no longer have access to high school counselors, have yet to engage with supports at their college, and typically cannot afford private college consulting.[4] And whereas middle- and upper-income parents tend to be heavily involved in the college process, lower-income parents may lack experience with the college process, and may be ill-equipped to provide guidance. Further, structural realities, such as the need for lower-income parents to work nonstandard hours or multiple jobs, may create barriers to regular routines at home and parents' ability to engage with their students on issues of college going.[5] Additionally, low-income parents may not believe their involvement would positively influence their children, or they may question whether the colleges allow for their involvement in the process.[6]

As a result, students who have already overcome many barriers to successful matriculation and appear to be on track for fall college matriculation at the time of high school graduation may nonetheless fail to enroll, a phenomenon to which we refer as "summer melt." Several studies document a substantial amount of summer attrition, up to 40 percent, among students who had been accepted to and intended to enroll in college as of high school graduation.[7] Encouragingly, we have also generated experimental evidence to illustrate that high school graduates' enrollment decisions are quite responsive to additional outreach and support during the post-high school summer. This outreach ranged from having school counselors or peer mentors proactively reach out to students during the summer to offer individualized guidance and assistance to a text messaging campaign in which students received personalized reminders of important tasks to complete at their intended institution. The interventions were comparatively low cost, from $7 to $200 per student, and increased college enrollment by 3–8 percentage points. By comparison, the financial aid literature has typically found that $1,000 in additional grant aid increases enrollment by 3–6 percentage points.[8]

In the remainder of this chapter, we first examine in greater detail why high school graduates who have surmounted many obstacles to college attainment may experience summer melt. We draw on various theoretical foundations to explain the high rates of summer attrition we have observed across settings. We then describe each of the interventions we have implemented to mitigate summer attrition. We focus on the behavioral mechanisms that each intervention is designed to address and highlight the main findings from each experiment.

Possible causes of summer melt

A number of factors may contribute to the failure of highly college-intending students to successfully matriculate during the fall following high school graduation. These factors relate to barriers to information as well as the complexity of college-related information that students and their families must process, aspects of adolescent development that are coincident to this period of college transition, and emerging theories in the field of behavioral economics about how individuals make decisions.

We begin by considering issues related to the complexity of college and financial aid information. Students and their families may have difficulty over the summer accessing, digesting, or completing various paperwork, such as supplementary loan applications and academic placement test registrations. A second consideration relates to how students respond behaviorally to the range of tasks they are expected to complete, particularly since they frequently lack access to professional guidance or support during the summer months. For instance, students may put off tasks that are particularly onerous or complex or struggle to keep track of deadlines associated with various responsibilities.

In addition, students may fail to realize their college intentions because they lack sufficient information about college costs and their options for financing postsecondary education, and are therefore unprepared to pay the tuition bill they receive midsummer. Several studies have documented that students and families from disadvantaged backgrounds often either struggle to estimate the cost of college tuition at all or substantially overestimate actual tuition expenses.[9] Specific to the context of the summer after high school graduation, students may lack information about their options for addressing financial gaps between their tuition bills and financial aid packages. Related to the credit constraint problem, students may be unaware that their parents can apply for supplemental loans from the federal government and that if parents' loan applications are rejected because of poor credit, the amount the student can borrow directly from the government automatically increases. Students may also be unaware that most colleges offer tuition payment plans that allow them to spread payments for the fall semester tuition bill over several months.[10]

An even more basic problem is that students from disadvantaged backgrounds may fail even to access their tuition bill or other important college information during the summer after high school. In recent years, many colleges have turned to web portals (for example, wolverineaccess.umich.edu) to disseminate key information to students. Students who are unfamiliar with the mechanics of these portals or who lack reliable Internet access over the summer may not receive many of the forms they are expected to complete in a timely fashion.[11]

NEW DIRECTIONS FOR YOUTH DEVELOPMENT • DOI: 10.1002.yd

Even among students who are able to access required college information over the summer, the complexity of paperwork students receive may impede their ability to complete all of the tasks necessary for successful matriculation. A number of studies document how high informational costs in the form of complexity can lead students to make suboptimal decisions about whether to apply for college or financial aid.[12] In the context of the summer after high school, students may struggle, for example, to distinguish grant aid from loan assistance on their financial aid award letters. They or their parents may be confused by the terms associated with supplemental loans they are considering, and students may be unsure about which other tasks, such as placement tests, they have to complete before versus during orientation.

A related point is that students may have difficulty visualizing the academic and social dimensions of college life—particularly if they have not had the opportunity to go on a campus visit. Aspiring first-generation college students, in particular, may lack a point of reference for the college experience; they do not know whether they will enjoy and thrive in the collegiate classroom; whether they will form new friendships; whether going to college will in fact result in a well-paying job. Faced with this uncertainty, students may be hesitant to relinquish the stability of their current lifestyle.[13]

A second set of considerations relates to the phase of development that coincides with the transition to postsecondary education and the implications that this has for the way that students respond behaviorally to college and financial aid tasks during the summer after high school. During the time period that students are engaged in the college choice process, they are in a phase of extensive cognitive development that impacts their reasoning, self-awareness, and ability to make decisions.[14] Neurological systems that respond to immediate stimulation are at their peak activity, yet brain systems required for self-regulation are still in development. As a result, adolescents are more impulsive, less likely to consider the long-term consequences of their present actions, and more likely to put off onerous tasks in favor of more pleasurable pursuits.[15] Given the cognitive transformations that adolescents experience in their late teens, when their organization, planning, and self-regulation capacities are in active development, completing tasks such as intricate college and financial aid processes that require substantial cognitive effort are likely to be particularly challenging for adolescents.

The complexity of decisions students face may also create considerable stress, undermining their confidence to make choices regarding their future.[16] This cognitive load may be particularly daunting for students from disadvantaged backgrounds who have to devote their time and energy to addressing immediate stressors, like supporting their families financially or dealing with neighborhood violence.[17] Faced with substantial time and cognitive burdens associated with accessing, digesting, and completing required college tasks over the summer, students may instead opt to put off, or abandon entirely, the tasks required for matriculation— particularly if the alternative activity is something more enticing, like spending time with friends. Individuals who highly discount future benefits relative to present costs are particularly likely to forego investments that require navigation of complex information and choices.[18]

A final set of considerations relates to students behavioral responses to required summer tasks. Students may fail to successfully matriculate in the fall because they fail to meet with key deadlines throughout the summer. Karlan, McConnell, Mullainathan, and Zinman develop a model in which limited attention can interfere with individuals' ability to moderate present consumption in anticipation of desired future actions or expenditures.[19] The authors posit that regular reminders should mitigate this "attentional failure" and help individuals smooth savings in preparation for a desired future expenditure. In many aspects of their academic lives, students are accustomed to such regular reminders. Throughout high school teachers provide students with frequent reminders of work they need to complete. In college, students receive syllabi detailing what to read each week and when assignments are due. High school students, even those from disadvantaged backgrounds, are exposed to an increasing range of school- and community-based

efforts to increase college going. For instance, 37 states participate in College Goal Sunday, which pairs students and families
with volunteers to help in applying for college or financial aid. Students from middle- and upper-class backgrounds receive frequent
prompts from their parents through the college application and
choice processes (see, for example, the November 30th, 2009 cover
story of *Time Magazine*: "The Case Against Over-Parenting").[20]
In contrast, for low-income and first-generation college students,
particularly those intending to enroll at large public institutions,
summer may be a uniquely "nudge"-free time.[21] Students may
not receive any personalized outreach reminding them of required
tasks.[22] In the absence of these nudges, students may miss important deadlines, such as registering for orientation, or have too little
time at the end of summer to complete everything that is required
of them.

Mitigating summer melt

Research from economics and psychology, among other disci-
plines, thus illustrates multiple factors that may contribute to why
strongly college-intending high school graduates may nonetheless fail to realize their college aspirations. Fortunately, this research also informs how interventions could be designed to mitigate summer attrition and increase college access among students
from disadvantaged backgrounds. Specifically, the literature suggests that low-income students would benefit from additional support to interpret and complete financial tasks and required college
paperwork. This support could come from a professional counselor or a peer mentor. Students could additionally benefit from
near-age peer support, since peers are uniquely positioned to provide first-hand, credible perspective and experience on overcom-
ing summer barriers to enrollment. Finally, students could benefit
from strategies that simplify and personalize the complex set of
information that students need to digest and to which they need
to respond in order to successfully matriculate at their intended

institution. We now turn to describing in greater detail three interventions we have implemented and assessed in order to understand the potential benefit of these types of summertime college-going supports.

In the first set of interventions, we investigated the impact of having school counselors or financial aid advisors reach out to college-intending high school graduates to offer additional support with college-related tasks. There are a variety of mechanisms by which the offer of counselor assistance could increase the probability of students' on-time transition to college. Counselors may be able to persuade students of the value of making short-term investments in higher education, given the longer-term benefits they are likely to realize. Counseling also should help students overcome the complexities in required paperwork they receive from their intended college. Finally, counselors may be able to help students devote time to task completion incrementally throughout the summer and therefore increase the probability that they are able to enroll.

During the summer of 2011, we collaborated with two educational agencies, uAspire and Fulton County Schools (FCS), to conduct summer counseling interventions.[23,24] uAspire is a Boston-based, nonprofit organization that provides college financial aid advising and scholarships to high school students.[25] FCS is a large urban school district in the metro-Atlanta area of Georgia with more than 90,000 students in 100 schools.

In each site, we randomly selected treatment group students to receive proactive outreach from a uAspire advisor or an FCS counselor over the course of the summer, while the control group students did not receive outreach.[26] Counselors made multiple attempts to contact each student in the treatment group to offer support and used a variety of communication methods. During the first in-person meeting, counselors completed a college-assessment protocol that we designed to achieve three purposes. First, counselors reviewed each student's financial aid award letter and provided guidance based on the student's level of unmet financial need. Second, counselors briefed the student on the calendar of key summer deadlines at the college the student planned to attend and helped the student understand and complete paperwork the student had already received from that college. Finally, the counselor assessed whether the student faced social or emotional barriers to fall college enrollment.[27]

At the conclusion of the assessment meeting, counselors helped students create a list of tasks required in order to start college that fall. Throughout the summer, counselors followed up with students individually to check on their progress with these tasks. Subsequent to the initial assessment meeting, much of the communication between counselors and students happened via phone, email, and text, though counselors also conducted in-person follow-up meetings with students when they felt it important to do so.

Our results indicate that college-intending high school graduates are responsive to the offer of summer counseling. Approximately half of the treatment group students in Boston met with an advisor at least once during the summer, compared with only 2 percent of students in the control group. The overall rate of counselor interaction in FCS was lower, close to one-third of treatment group students, but there were substantial differences in take-up by whether students qualified for free- or reduced-price lunch (FRL). Whereas only a quarter of non-FRL students in the treatment group interacted with an FCS counselor over the summer, over half of FRL students did so.

Further, the offer of summer counseling support had a strong, positive impact on both college enrollment and persistence for students overall in Boston and a particularly pronounced impact for FRL-eligible students in FCS. Students in Boston who were offered a few hours of additional counseling assistance were over 5 percentage points more likely to enroll in the fall semester following high school compared to students who were not offered additional assistance. In Fulton County, the impact of summer counseling on fall enrollment was even greater for FRL students, for whom the summer outreach improved fall college enrollment by almost 8 percentage points.

Even more pronounced were the impacts on persistence: in Boston, students who were offered additional summer counseling were almost 7 percentage points more likely to persist into the spring of freshman year in college and almost 9 percentage points more likely to persist into the fall semester of sophomore year in college than students who were not offered assistance.[28] These persistence impacts are particularly important. One potential criticism of offering students additional support after high school graduation is that students who struggle to access and complete required paperwork during the summer are unlikely to possess the skills, either academic or problem solving, necessary for success in the classroom and perseverance in college. These persistence impacts suggest that the challenges students encounter over the summer may not relate directly to their ability to succeed in college.

Given the positive effects we observe, an important question is what mechanisms are driving these impacts? Based on a set of follow-up focus groups and interviews with counselors and students in Boston on which we collaborated with Karen Arnold of Boston College, several themes emerged: A key part of the story is that advisors helped students reduce college costs to the point that they could afford to enroll. Counselors helped students to qualify for aid if they had not already, to waive costs where possible (for example, waiving their college's health insurance plan in favor of their parents' coverage), to sign up for tuition payment plans to spread payments over several months, and, if necessary, to select a more affordable college to attend. Helping students access information appears to have been another important element of the summer support. For instance, many counselors reported helping students access and navigate the college web portals through which colleges now disseminate substantial information over the summer, but with which students were often unfamiliar. Finally, an important part of the summer work is providing students with nudges to complete required tasks. As one counselor said, they were essentially filling in for what middle-class parents would do with their own children—providing the necessary guidance and reminders that students' parents were unable to offer for lack of first-hand experience.

In reflecting on these counselor-led interventions and how they might be replicated and expanded, several questions emerged about how to most effectively provide students with support during this time period. One question is to whose offer of help students are most likely to respond. During summer 2011, we had worked with high school counselors and community-based financial aid advisors. Might college-aged peer mentors from the same high schools who can share first-hand experiences of how they navigated summer obstacles and managed to succeed in college be as or more effective in providing outreach and support? On the one hand, peer mentors could potentially be more effective at making contact with students; on the other hand, they may not have the same impact on whether students actually enrolled, for lack of sufficient training or counseling expertise. Finally, how important is personal outreach (for example, a phone call from a counselor) versus personalized outreach? Counselors reported investing considerable time just trying to reach students and get them in the door to meet. What if we could automate and personalize outreach and, at the same time, share information specific to students' intended college?

In summer 2012, we collaborated with Laura Owen at Johns Hopkins University, Bridget Terry Long at Harvard University, and Eric Bettinger at Stanford University, to implement a broader set of college-going interventions through which we launched three follow-up randomized trials. Through one intervention, students were enrolled in a text message campaign through which they received personalized reminders of required college tasks and the offer of one-on-one help from a school counselor. Through another intervention, we hired peer mentors to reach out to students, to offer them help, first-hand perspective and encouragement, and to connect them to professional staff if they needed additional assistance. Finally, in the third intervention, we facilitated a partnership between a large southwestern urban school district and the university where the majority of college-bound graduates from the district enroll, to investigate whether outreach from the high school or college side differentially impacts whether students enroll. In sum, we worked with eight large urban districts across the country, with a total experimental sample of approximately 12,500 students. Our analyses of the APS-UNM intervention are still ongoing, so we focus in the remainder of the paper on the design of and results from the text message and peer mentor interventions.[29]

The potential of text messaging to deliver personalized college information

For several reasons, text messaging is a promising means of delivering personalized college information to students and facilitating connections to school counselors. Texting is the predominant means by which young people communicate. Whereas only 6 percent of teens exchange emails and 39 percent talk via mobile phones, 63 percent send texts on a daily basis.[30] Moreover, a text campaign may increase the efficiency of school counselors' time. With a text platform, message delivery can be *automated* and *personalized* to individual students and their postsecondary plans, eliminating the need for counselors to invest substantial time in conducting outreach and instead allowing them to focus efforts on providing guidance where needed. Finally, both public health and development economics research reveals positive impacts of text messaging campaigns on desired outcomes, such as whether individuals contribute regularly to a savings account or get a flu vaccination.[31]

Personalized text messages could positively impact successful fall matriculation among college-intending students via several possible mechanisms. As noted above, text messaging may efficiently connect students to school counselors who can provide help to address summer obstacles to enrollment. Enabling students to request assistance via text message minimizes several potential barriers to help-seeking. For instance, in under-resourced schools where counselors have large caseloads and minimal time to focus on college planning, high school graduates may have had limited personal relationships with counselors.[32] Given this lack of personal connection, recent graduates may not view their high school counselor as an obvious source of support or may be inhibited more generally from initiating contact. Receiving proactive outreach and taking up the offer of assistance by responding to a text message, in contrast, may require considerably less interpersonal effort.

Personalized text messages may also improve rates of college matriculation by informing students of required summer tasks about which they were previously unaware and/or by simplifying the steps required to complete these tasks. Particularly as colleges have favored online dissemination of information, students may struggle to comprehensively identify the tasks and associated deadlines required to successfully matriculate. A text message campaign can be implemented to provide students with institution- and task-specific information together with links to web pages relevant to completing a given task (for example, registering for orientation).

Finally, the text outreach may positively impact college outcomes simply by nudging students to complete required tasks by the relevant deadline. In this way, personalized messaging may effectively turn adolescents' greatest liability—their impulsiveness—into an asset.[33] By providing simplified information and college- and task-specific links, each message allows completion of required steps in the moment, before students' attention is diverted elsewhere.

The potential of peer mentoring to mitigate summer attrition

Peer mentoring is another promising strategy to increase college going among low-income high school graduates. First, high school graduates may be more responsive to summer outreach from peers than from adults who make similar efforts. Peer mentors are also more likely to be facile with modes of communication that are common among recent high school graduates, and peer mentors may be uniquely effective at positively altering students' perceptions of social norms regarding college. Near-age peer mentors who are from similar backgrounds, who graduated from proximate high schools, and who are currently thriving in college may be uniquely poised to shift recent high school graduates' conceptions about who goes to and succeeds in college. To the extent that this change in perspective reduces the psychic costs associated with college, students may be more likely to complete required summer tasks and/or seek out individualized assistance when needed in order to matriculate.

Peer mentors may also increase the probability that students matriculate by concretizing the potential benefits of college. Time and travel costs may prevent students from visiting their intended college campus, and first-generation college students who received little prior college counseling may struggle to visualize college life. As a result, students may have less access to information about the benefits of college than traditional human capital investment models would posit. Students may accordingly be averse to forego current situations in favor of an unfamiliar environment.[34] Therefore, peer mentors may help to solidify students' perceptions of what college has to offer. Especially when peer mentors are from similar age, racial/ethnic, and gender groups, students may find their perspective and experience particularly salient.[35]

Sites and intervention design

During the summer of 2012, we collaborated with the Dallas Independent School District (Dallas ISD), uAspire, and Mastery Charter Schools, a network of charter schools in the Philadelphia metropolitan area (Mastery) to conduct the text message and peer mentor interventions. We implemented the text message intervention with both Dallas and uAspire and the peer mentor

NEW DIRECTIONS FOR YOUTH DEVELOPMENT • DOI: 10.1002.yd

intervention with uAspire and Mastery. In addition to its Boston location, uAspire operates in the Massachusetts school districts of Lawrence and Springfield. We worked with all three sites for the text message and peer mentor interventions. Dallas ISD is a large, urban school district, serving approximately 158,000 students across 227 high schools, and Mastery Charter Schools serve approximately 8,000 students in grades kindergarten through 12.

The core of the text campaign was a series of 8–10 text messages that reminded students and their parents of key tasks to complete for their intended college and that offered recipients the opportunity to meet with a school counselor from their district if they needed additional assistance.[36] More specifically, the messages reminded students to: log on to their intended college's web portal (for example, wolverineaccess.umich.edu) to access important paperwork, to register for orientation and placement tests, to complete housing forms, and to sign up for or waive health insurance, if relevant. The messages also offered students the opportunity to obtain help in completing the FAFSA, if they had not done so already, and help in interpreting their financial aid award letter and tuition bill. Most messages included web links that allowed students to complete tasks directly from their phone (if they had a smart phone and a data plan).[37] The text messages were delivered between early July and mid-August in approximately five-day intervals.

The peer mentor intervention built largely on the counselor-led outreach interventions described above. The primary difference with the peer mentor intervention was that college students who had graduated from public high schools in each uAspire site or from a Mastery high school were conducting the initial outreach to students and providing the first level of support and guidance, with supervision from a professional counselor.

Peer mentors had several goals in their initial outreach to students. Their primary task was to make contact with students and assess their readiness for fall college matriculation. Some of the core topics that peer mentors covered in their initial conversation were whether the student was still planning to enroll in college, and if so, at the college indicated at the end of senior year, had completed the FAFSA, had received and reviewed a financial aid award letter, and had registered for orientation and placement tests. Following this initial assessment, peer mentors held in-person meetings or follow-up phone conversations to assist with issues that arose during the initial conversations. For instance, peer mentors helped students interpret their financial aid award letters and explore tuition payment plan options. Peer mentors also reviewed the briefing documents for the colleges and universities frequently attended by graduates at participating sites and helped students identify tasks they had yet to complete.

Peer mentors did not, however, directly support tasks that required students to provide financial information about themselves or their families, such as completing the FAFSA or applying for supplementary loans. For these tasks as well as other areas in which the peer mentor did not feel suitably equipped to comprehensively provide support, peer mentors referred students to a supervising counselor.

The text messaging and peer mentor outreach campaigns both had a positive impact on whether college-intending high school graduates enrolled in college. Text outreach increased enrollment in two-year institutions by over 3 percentage points, while peer mentor outreach increased four-year enrollment by nearly 5 percentage points. These overall results mask considerable impact heterogeneity which begins to shed light on for whom and the conditions under which these types of interventions may be particularly beneficial. The impacts in Dallas, for example, were concentrated among students who qualified for FRL and students who fell in the middle of the achievement distribution as measured by GPA and standardized test performance. In Lawrence and Springfield, Massachusetts, students in the text message treatment group were 7 percentage points more likely to enroll in college, with this impact equally divided between enrollment at four-year and two-year institutions. The peer mentor impacts in Lawrence and Springfield were largest among males, and across the uAspire sites, both text and peer mentor impacts were largest among students who began the summer without specifically articulated postsecondary plans.

Taken collectively, these results suggest that the text intervention was most impactful for students who plausibly had less access to college and financial aid information, either because they were from communities with low educational attainment and few college-going supports, or because they themselves were from socioeconomically disadvantaged families. Both the text and peer mentor interventions had pronounced effects on students who began the summer with less-solidified college plans, and who therefore could have benefited from additional guidance of tasks to complete. Finally, the peer mentor intervention was quite effective for male students; one reason for this may be that student-mentor matching was largely done along gender lines. Particularly given broad concerns about gender disparities in educational achievement and attainment, the peer mentor results offer a promising approach for increasing college access among males from disadvantaged backgrounds.

Perhaps the most striking feature of the interventions, and the text messaging intervention, in particular, is their cost effectiveness. Including the cost of up-front system design and the per-message delivery charges, the total messaging cost per student in the Dallas and uAspire treatment groups was approximately $2, or roughly $5,000 across both sites. The other primary expense was compensation for counselors to staff the summer intervention, which raised the per-student cost of the intervention to a mere $7. The costs of the peer mentor intervention were primarily hourly wages to the peer mentors themselves and salary for supervising advisors, which totaled approximately $80 per student. This is more similar in cost to counselor-led interventions. Given the magnitude of the impacts we observe per dollar spent, both interventions appear considerably more cost effective than other strategies to increase college access among students from disadvantaged backgrounds (for example, giving students additional grant aid).

Conclusion

In sum, college-intending, low-income high school graduates face a host of informational, financial, and other barriers to enrollment that may prevent them from successfully matriculating. Encouragingly, the experimental evidence that we have generated indicates that for these same students, proactive outreach by counselors, peer mentors, or even via text message during this period can lead to substantial improvements in rates of on-time college graduation. These findings have significant implications for policy, practice, and research. Gaps in college enrollment and success by socioeconomic status have persisted for decades and have widened among recent cohorts.[38] School districts are under mounting pressure to improve college-going rates among underrepresented populations, yet they often have limited resources with which to invest in initiatives targeted to these outcomes. At a time when the private and social returns to a college education are particularly high, yet district, state, and federal budgets are especially lean, we conclude that proactively reaching out to students over the summer to provide them with information, encouragement, and individualized assistance represents a cost-effective approach to increasing college access among low-income students who aspire to further their education.

Notes

1. Cooper, H., Nye, B., Charlton, K., Lindsay, J., & Greathouse, S. (1996). The effects of summer vacation on achievement test scores: A narrative and meta-analytic review. *Review of Educational Research*, 66, 227–268; Entwisle, D. R., Alexander, K. L., & Olson, L. S. (1997). *Children, schools, and inequality.* Boulder, CO: Westview Press.

2. Hossler, D., & Gallagher, K. S. (1987). Studying student college choice: A three-phase model and the implications for policymakers. *College and University*, 62(3), 207–221.

3. Arnold, K. C., Fleming, S., DeAnda, M., Castleman, B. L., & Wartman, K. L. (2009). The summer flood: The invisible gap among low-income students. *Thought and Action, Fall, 2009*, 23–34; Castleman, B. L., Arnold, K. C., & Wartman, K. L. (2012a). Stemming the tide of summer melt: An experimental study of the effects of post-high school summer intervention on

low-income students' college enrollment. *The Journal of Research on Educational Effectiveness*, *5*(1), 1–18; Castleman, B. L., Page, L. C., & Schooley, K. (in press). The forgotten summer: The impact of college counseling the summer after high school on whether students enroll in college. *Journal of Policy Analysis and Management*.

4. Arnold et al. (2009); Castleman et al. (2012a); Castleman et al. (in press).

5. Acs, G. & Loprest, P. J. (2005). *Who are low-income working families?* Washington, DC: The Urban Institute; Hsueh, J., & Yoshikawa, H. (2007). Working nonstandard schedules and variable shifts in low-income families: Associations with parental psychological well-being, family functioning, and child well-being. *Developmental Psychology*, *43*, 620–632; Presser, H. B., & Cox, A. G. (1997). The work schedules of low-educated American women and welfare reform. *Monthly Labor Review*, *4*(120), 25–34.

6. Perna, L. W. (2004). Understanding the decision to enroll in graduate school: Sex and racial/ethnic group differences. *Journal of Higher Education*, *75*, 487–527; Rowan-Kenyon, H. T., Bell, A., & Perna, L. W. (2008). Contextual influences on parental involvement in college going: Variations by socioeconomic class. *Journal of Higher Education*, *79*, 564–586.

7. Castleman, B. L., & Page, L. C. (2013). A trickle or a torrent? Understanding the extent of summer "melt" among college-intending high school graduates. *Social Sciences Quarterly*. doi:10.1111/ssqu.12032; Daugherty, L. (2011). *An evaluation of Summer Link, a counseling program to facilitate college-going*. Paper presented at the Annual Meeting of the Association for Public Policy Analysis and Management, Washington, DC; Matthews, C., Schooley, K, & Vosler, N. (2011, February 14). *Proposal for a Summer Transition Program to increase FCS college-going rates*. Fulton County, GA: Fulton County Schools.

8. Deming, D., & Dynarski, S. M. (2009). *Into college, out of poverty? Policies to increase the postsecondary attainment of the poor* (NBER Working Paper No. 15387). Cambridge, MA: National Bureau of Economic Research.

9. Avery, C., & Kane, T. J. (2004). Student perceptions of college opportunities. The Boston COACH program. In C. Hoxby (Ed.), *College choices: The economics of where to go, when to go, and how to pay for it* (pp. 355–394). Chicago, IL: University of Chicago Press; Horn, L., Chen, X., & Chapman, C. (2003). *Getting ready to pay for college: What students and their parents know about the cost of college tuition and what they are doing to find out*. Washington, DC: U.S. Department of Education, National Center for Education Statistics; Grodsky, E., & Jones, M. T. (2007). Real and imagined barriers to college entry: Perceptions of cost. *Social Science Research*, *36*(2), 745–766.

10. Arnold, K. C., Chewning, A., Castleman, B. L., & Page, L. C. (2013). *Advisor and student experiences of summer support for college-intending, low-income high school graduates*. Paper presented at the Annual Meeting of the Association for the Study of Higher Education, St. Louis, MO.

11. Castleman et al. (in press).

12. Avery & Kane (2004); Bettinger, E., Long, B. T., Oreopoulos, P., & Sanbonmatsu, L. (2012). The role of application assistance and information in college decisions: Results from the H&R Block FAFSA experiment. *Quarterly Journal of Economics*, *127*(3), 1205–1242; Dynarski, S. M., & Scott-Clayton,

J. E. (2006). The cost of complexity in federal student aid: Lessons from optimal tax theory and behavioral economics. *National Tax Journal, 59*(2), 319–356.

13. Kahneman, D., & Tversky, A. (1979). Prospect theory: An analysis of decision under risk. *Econometrica, 47*(2), 263–291.

14. Keating, D. P. (2004). Cognitive and brain development. In R. M. Lerner & L. Steinberg (Eds.), *Handbook of adolescent psychology* (2nd ed., pp. 45–84). New York, NY: Wiley.

15. Casey, B., Jones, R. M., & Somerville, L. H. (2011). Braking and accelerating of the adolescent brain. *Journal of Research on Adolescence, 21*(1), 21–33; Steinberg, L. (2008). A social neuroscience perspective on adolescent risk-taking. *Development Review, 28*, 78–106; Steinberg, L., Cauffman, E., Woolard, J., Graham, S., & Banich, M. (2009). Are adolescents less mature than adults? Minors' access to abortion, the juvenile death penalty, and the alleged APA "Flip-Flop." *American Psychologist, 64*, 583–594.

16. Schneider, B. (2009). *College choice and adolescent development: Psychological and social implications of early admission.* Arlington, VA: National Association for College Admissions Counseling.

17. Mullainathan, S. (2011). The psychology of poverty. *Focus, 28*(1), 19–22.

18. Madrian, B. C., & Shea, D. F. (2000). *The power of suggestion: Inertia in 401(K) participation and savings behavior* (NBER Working Paper No. 7682). Cambridge, MA: National Bureau of Economic Research Working Paper; Beshears, J., Choi, J. J., Laibson, D., & Madrian, B. C. (2012). *Simplification and saving* (NBER Working Paper No. 12659). Cambridge, MA: National Bureau of Economic Research; Scott-Clayton, J. (2011). *The shapeless river: Does a lack of structure inhibit students' progress community colleges?* (CCRC Working Paper No. 25). New York, NY: Community College Research Center, Teachers College, Columbia University.

19. Karlan, D., McConnell, M., Mullainathan, S., & Zinman, J. (2010). *Getting to the top of mind: How reminders increase saving* (NBER Working Paper No. 16205). Cambridge, MA: National Bureau of Economic Research

20. Gibbs, N. (2009, November 30). The growing backlash against overparenting. *Time Magazine.*

21. Thaler, R., & Sunstein, C. (2008). *Nudge: Improving decisions about health, wealth, and happiness.* New Haven, CT: Yale University Press.

22. Arnold et al. (2009). Pp. 23–24.

23. These interventions were based on a successful pilot experiment we ran in Providence, RI, in summer 2008. For more information on this pilot, see Castleman et al. (2012a).

24. For additional details on the design, implementation, and results of the summer 2011 counseling interventions in Boston and Fulton County, GA, see Castleman et al. (in press).

25. More information about uAspire can be found at www.uaspireusa.org

26. In Boston, treatment and control group students alike were told prior to the start of the intervention that individualized counseling would be available from uAspire over the summer. In FCS, students were not made

aware of the program prior to its commencement. In either site, control group students who initiated contact received the same level of support as those in the treatment group.

27. Materials we developed to guide counselors' interactions with students are available upon request.

28. To date, we have not be able to observe students' enrollment over a longer time horizon.

29. For additional details on the design, implementation, and results of the summer 2012 text message and peer mentor interventions, see Castleman and Page (2013).

30. Lenhardt, A. (2012). *Teens, smart phones, and texting.* Washington, DC: Pew Research Center.

31. Karlan et al. (2010); Stockwell, M. S., Kharbanda, E. O., Martinez, R. A., Vargas, C. Y., Vawdrey, D. K., & Camargo, S. (2012). Effects of a text messaging intervention on influenza vaccination in an urban, low-income pediatric and adolescent population. *Journal of the American Medical Association, 307*(16), 1702–1708.

32. Civic Enterprises (2012). *School counselors literature and landscape review.* New York, NY: Civic Enterprises for the College Board.

33. We are grateful to Tom Kane for making this point.

34. Kahneman & Tversky (1979).

35. Cialdini, R. B., & Goldstein, N. J. (2004). Social influence: Compliance and conformity. *Annual Review of Psychology, 55,* 591–621; Murray, D. M., Luepker, R. V., Johnson, A. C., & Mittelmark, M. B. (1984). The prevention of cigarette smoking in children: A comparison of four strategies. *Journal of Applied Social Psychology, 14*(3), 274–88; White, K. M., Hogg, M. A., & Terry, D. J. (2002). Improving attitude-behavior correspondence through exposure to normative support from a salient in-group. *Basic and Applied Social Psychology,* (24), 91–103.

36. Students who were planning to attend a less common institution received a generic set of reminders.

37. Message content is available upon request.

38. Bailey, M. J., & Dynarski, S. M. (2012). *Gains and gaps; Changing inequality in U.S. college entry and completion* (NBER Working Paper No. 17633). Cambridge, MA: National Bureau of Economic Research.

BENJAMIN L. CASTLEMAN *is an assistant professor of education and public policy at the University of Virginia.*

LINDSAY C. PAGE *is a research assistant professor at the University of Pittsburgh School of Education.*

Promise scholarships offer an alternative to traditional aid programs by making commitments to students early on in high school and providing motivation and encouragement as students prepare for college.

5

Is traditional financial aid too little, too late to help youth succeed in college? An introduction to *The Degree Project* promise scholarship experiment

Douglas N. Harris

ONE OF THE MAIN purposes of education, and a primary reason for government funding, is to provide opportunities to people across all walks of life—to level the playing field of life chances. By almost all accounts, however, the system fails miserably. Children from low-income families are much less likely than their higher-income peers, as Heckman and his colleagues argue, to enter or graduate from college.[1] Compared with the lowest income quartile, students in the highest income quartile are almost three times and likely to enter college and six times as likely to complete a bachelor's degree.[2] This is especially troubling given the rising return to education and other social benefits of higher education.[3]

One theory is that low-income students do not succeed in college because they are less academically prepared at the end of high school.[4] But inequality in academic preparation cannot be the only

NEW DIRECTIONS FOR YOUTH DEVELOPMENT, NO. 140, WINTER 2013 © WILEY PERIODICALS, INC.
Published online in Wiley Online Library (wileyonlinelibrary.com) • DOI: 10.1002/yd.20080

explanation.[5] One-third of the income gap in college entry cannot be explained by cognitive skills and high-income students with low test scores are about as likely to attend college as low-income students with high test scores.[6]

An additional potential cause of the income gap in college outcomes may be the rising price of college.[7] For more than a century, college tuition has risen at a rate of 2–3 percentage points above the rate of inflation and in recent years it has risen much faster than real median income.[8] This has contributed to a 350 percent increase in loans.[9]

While these rising costs have been largely offset by increased government financial aid for low-income students, there are still some ways in which low-income groups have been harder hit.[10] Compared with more advantaged groups, they seem to be more averse to taking out loans and overstate college costs by a factor of three.[11] Low-income students also express concern about the cost of college—in our own data, students report this as one of the greatest barriers to college success.

Given the concerns about costs, it is perhaps somewhat surprising that financial aid programs seem to be only moderately cost effective in helping students persist in college through graduation. Students do slightly better with more aid, but at considerable expense.[12] These findings have brought renewed interest to the design of financial aid. Are there better ways to use aid to address rising costs, especially for low-income groups? Many researchers seem to think so and have proposed ways to redesign these programs, for example, by simplifying and easing the burden of financial aid forms.[13]

Another problem—and the focus of this chapter—is that traditional aid programs do not make concrete commitments to students until they are nearly finished with high school, when many are already off track. The concern over cost and affordability might make students less likely to work hard in school or see themselves as college material. There is another way. "Promise scholarships" make commitments to low-income students when they are much younger and therefore have the potential to encourage students to better prepare during high school, develop the social capital they need to navigate the path to college, and pay for growing college costs—and at very little additional cost.

Promise programs might help build a road to college—by providing some gas money—with which students can "drive" their strong college aspirations. At least seventy-three such programs exist nationally, including the well-known *Kalamazoo Promise*, and have received wide national media and political attention.[14] In a speech at a high school that had such a program, President Obama spoke about how the early aid had "helped inspire an entire generation of young people here . . . to imagine a different future for themselves."[15]

Unfortunately, the praise has somewhat outpaced the evidence. In this chapter, we describe the design and rationale for *The Degree Project* (TDP), the first U.S. randomized trial of a promise scholarship. In addition to the important new evidence the demonstration program will generate, TDP also shows how educators and researchers can work together to provide the insight and answers policy makers need to address very real education gaps. After discussing the program and setting in more detail, we elaborate on the rationale and discuss potential policy implications.

The Degree Project (TDP)

On November 17, 2011, all first-time ninth graders attending half of Milwaukee's thirty-six public ninth-grade schools were given the chance to receive $12,000 to pay for college. The Great Lakes Higher Education Corporation (Great Lakes) has committed up to $31 million to fund the scholarships, enough to provide the full scholarship to every one of the 2,587 TDP promise recipients.

To receive the money, students will have to meet some academic and other requirements during high school and of course eventually attend college. While there are not explicit income requirements, 82 percent of MPS students are eligible for free- or reduced-price lunches. Only 69 percent of MPS ninth graders typically complete high school on time and only 44 percent of those high school graduates directly transition to college.[16]

Students will receive TDP funds so long as they graduate on time with at least a 2.5 cumulative GPA (C+/B−) and attend class 90% of the time.[17] To graduate, students must meet MPS academic requirements and GEDs do not qualify. In addition, TDP scholarships will require students to complete a Free Application for Federal Student Aid (FAFSA) during their senior year and each year of college, and attend an eligible college at least half-time. The GPA and attendance requirements—nearly identical to those of the *Pittsburgh Promise*—are cumulative across years, so that students who fall behind can catch up.

TDP scholarships must be used within four years of expected high school graduation. Students need not start college immediately, but must start within fifteen months of on-time high school graduation. For example, students who do not attend college at all in the first year after high school graduation can still use the full scholarship amount, but they would have to do so by spring 2019. The college must be one of the sixty-six public or nonprofit two- or four-year institutions in Wisconsin, a list that includes almost all of those commonly attended by MPS graduates. There are no GPA requirements during college.[18]

TDP scholarships are "last dollar" and will cover up to the cost of attendance. Many TDP students will have a zero expected family contribution (zero EFC); for these students, the total TDP scholarship would cover the entire cost of attendance for more than two years at a public two-year college. Looking at the full-time tuition and fees of the two- and four-year institutions most commonly attended by MPS students—$3,184 annually at Milwaukee Area Technical College (MATC) and $8,675 annually at the University of Wisconsin–Milwaukee (UW–Milwaukee)—we see that TDP by itself would cover all tuition and fees for a two-year degree and more than one full year at a four-year college. (Half of MPS students who go on to college attend one of these two institutions.) Although tuition and fees are likely to rise before 2015, when TDP recipients first enter college, $12,000 constitutes a substantial reduction in the direct costs of college, and perhaps more importantly, will likely seem a large amount of money to a ninth grader.

TDP communications plan

Information is crucial to the success of almost any program, and especially those that involve financial incentives with eligibility requirements, involving disadvantaged groups. For that reason, the program funder is carrying out an aggressive communication plan. Prior research suggests that students are ill-informed about the steps they have to take to be successful in college, especially about costs and financial aid.[19] Even when they are already receiving aid, students often forget about the opportunities available to them.[20]

Therefore, three months after the initial announcement, Great Lakes sent individualized reminder letters that indicated whether each student was "on track" to meet the requirements. These on-track letters will be sent approximately three times per year during high school. As with the initial award letters, all on-track letters and subsequent written communication will be sent twice, one to school and one home by U.S. Mail.

Going forward, these letters will also include information about typical high school course work of successful college students, average college costs and financial aid amounts in Wisconsin, names of colleges recently attended by MPS students, and the process for—and importance of—signing up for the ACT test. Because one requirement is filling out the FAFSA, the program will provide FAFSA information to students multiple times as they begin their senior year. Research shows that FAFSA completion is a significant impediment to college entry.[21] Finally, the program has a public web site (www.degreeproject.com) and a telephone hotline to address questions.

Random assignment

In addition to the careful design of the program itself, TDP was designed to provide the most convincing evidence possible about its cost effectiveness. The eighteen schools where first-time ninth graders received the scholarship offer were therefore selected *at random* and the remaining eighteen schools serve as the control group. This type of experiment, or randomized controlled trial, is generally considered the most rigorous method for identifying the effects of almost any program.[22] Because schools were chosen for the scholarship offer at random and have an equal chance of being chosen, we can expect that, in the absence of the scholarship, the two groups would have had the same high school and college outcomes—the same grades, attendance, and college completion. Therefore, any differences in outcomes must be due to TDP. In contrast, in Kalamazoo, the absence of random assignment and other factors led its evaluators to conclude that "it is difficult to determine how much of [the effects] can be attributed to the Promise versus other changes."[23]

In most experiments, students are selected so that some within the same classroom or school receive the treatment and others do not. This "individual randomization" is a problem in cases where, as with TDP, the treatment might have a positive feedback loop across students. For example, if TDP increases college expectations for one student, that might carry over to higher expectations for that student's friends and peers. But if we had randomized individuals so that some students in each ninth-grade class received the treatment and others not, the feedback loop—or "spillovers"—would not have as much of a chance to work and we would have misunderstood how the program would work if applied to all students and schools.[24] The fact that whole groups of students were

Figure 5.1. Theory of change

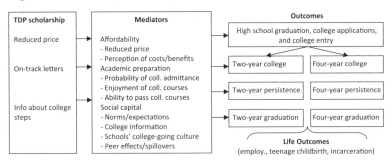

chosen for TDP—all first-time ninth graders in eighteen schools—is therefore significant, and more like the natural implementation of government programs. Large groups of students (around 140 on average per school) in the same school will experience TDP at the same time and the benefits for each may add to the benefits for all.

General rationale: Affordability, social capital, and academic preparation

Our general rationale for early aid programs like TDP, compared with traditional "late commitment" aid, is that early aid will reduce students' concern and uncertainty about college costs and therefore encourage them to better prepare during high school. Here, we explain in greater detail by breaking down TDP into its three components: the reduced price of college that comes with the potential $12,000, the on-track letters, and other information about the key steps to college success sent by Great Lakes.

Our theory, as shown in Figure 5.1, is that all three of these are important and collectively result in improved affordability, better academic preparation, and increased social capital.[25] While the three program components are interdependent, the three arrows on the left side of Figure 5.1 suggest the primary influences of each component. For example, the primary effect of the scholarship offer is to make college more affordable (first arrow); also, by

NEW DIRECTIONS FOR YOUTH DEVELOPMENT • DOI: 10.1002.yd

reminding students of their academic success with the on-track let-ters, students may be motivated to improve their academic prepa-ration (second arrow).

Finally, we believe the additional information we provide about college, combined with the potential feedback loop, will facili-tate social capital formation (third arrow). For instance, the col-lege information provided by TDP will help do the work that counselors often cannot do themselves, initiating additional stu-dent–counselor interactions and establishing norms of college-going that are accepted by students and counselors. These student–counselor interactions may add up to more than the sum of their parts, creating a stronger college-going school culture.

The outcomes are listed on the right side of Figure 5.1. Re-search suggests that many of the same general factors affecting col-lege entry also affect persistence and completion, for example, af-fordability and academic preparation.[26] In fact, as researchers have found, students appear to drop out because they have chosen col-leges that are less competitive than their skills warrant—they are "under-matched."[27] Academically prepared students often never even apply to colleges commensurate with their ability, partly be-cause of the college-going culture of the school.[28] Affordability, academic preparation, and social capital may each have different effects on entry versus persistence in college. For this reason, we list each of the four main college outcomes separately and allow separate paths/mechanisms for each outcome. Finally, improved education outcomes may, in turn, increase employment and reduce teenage childbirth and incarceration. Our ongoing analysis of the TDP will examine all of these outcomes.

Figure 5.1 oversimplifies matters in at least one important way. We view the decision to go to college—and acquire academic and social capital—as the result of complex and interrelated processes. For example, academic preparation could be influenced by either the increased affordability of college (college is more likely and in-duces students to work harder to be ready for it) and/or by the GPA and attendance requirements (some students would go to college anyway, but the requirements still induce them to work harder). These complex processes—which are difficult to illustrate with boxes and arrows—become more evident as we elaborate on the theoretical model and discuss below existing evidence about promise programs.

Affordability. Basic economic theory suggests that promise programs, as well as other forms of financial aid, increase the likelihood of college success simply by making it less expensive.[29] While students often seem responsive to costs, tuition, and financial aid, they do not act like "adolescent econometricians," as Manski points out, and do not make education decisions in ways predicted by basic economic theory.[30] Part of the problem is that students misperceive the costs and benefits of college. TDP will address affordability by providing substantial funds and by communicating with students and parents about college costs. We are aware of no prior evidence about how students' perceptions about college costs are affected by promise programs.

Academic preparation. A substantial literature indicates the importance of academic preparation—specifically, preparation for college-level courses.[31] Some researchers of college readiness have stressed the need to develop basic skills in reading and writing, content-specific academic skills, and noncognitive skills, such as perseverance. This may be why college financial aid programs with performance requirements appear to be more effective than those that do not.[32] TDP could improve academic preparation with its GPA and class attendance requirements and by communicating the academic path to college.

Evidence about effects of U.S. promise programs on high school academic outcomes is positive, but not very persuasive. In studying the *Kalamazoo Promise*, which provides up to 100 percent tuition for each graduate of the public schools, Bartik, Eberts, and Huang report that student achievement increased considerably in Kalamazoo, MI schools after the Kalamazoo Promise was instituted and that 30 percent of students said that they had enrolled in more college preparation courses during high school because of the promise.[33] Also, 58 percent of the students interviewed and 66 percent of the school employees believed that students' attitudes about school work had improved.[34] Again, whether these studies really reflect the effects of the programs is questionable because of the lack of random assignment or other methods to convincingly account for student differences.

More recent evidence from Kalamazoo is mixed. Bartik and Lachowska report a small positive effect on GPA and one fewer suspension day per year.[35] On the other hand, there were no effects on the number of suspensions, suggesting that the effect on suspensions may be due to school principals being more lenient in punishing scholarship-eligible students. Also, another recent report suggests that high school graduation rates for minorities have been unchanged since the start of the Kalamazoo Promise.

Social capital. Social capital can be defined in different ways, but in this case we focus on social norms and information available to students and their capacity to navigate the bureaucratic processes pertaining to college. Limited access to these forms of social capital is likely to be a key factor preventing students from reaching their college potential, but the key policy issue is to what degree educational policy can address this mechanism.[36]

Students' peers represent one important social network and have been shown to play an important role in college access.[37] I have written elsewhere about the complexity of peer interactions in general and surveyed a range of theories to explain them.[38] Building on prior work, I argued that the evidence favors a theory of *group-based contagion*—that is, students tend to emulate the specific peers with whom they identify most closely, such as those of the same race or gender.[39] Thus, if getting a TDP scholarship can directly influence the information and beliefs of individual students, then this could have positive spillovers for their classmates and friends in terms of group information and social norms around college going.

School teachers and counselors can also be viewed as sources of social capital. Some research shows that students need "structures of support" to help them navigate the college selection, admission, and financial aid processes.[40] Educators, along with peers, also help to establish a college-going culture that sets a norm of college entry.[41] This finding highlights how social capital and academic preparation are intertwined. A college-going culture, for example, may induce students to take more demanding courses and study harder. Further, if college-going becomes more the norm, then students may gather more college information and share that through their social networks, so that peers and counselors help to offset limited social capital in students' families.

Even if financial aid does not affect short-term behavior, it may change students' perceptions and expectations in ways that influence future behavior. Psychological theory and research suggest that expectations and students' perceived control over college opportunities are affected by costs and financial aid and are strong predictors of college success, even after accounting for a host of other observable differences.[42] While college expectations are generally high among adolescents, low-income groups have lower expectations that decline sooner and faster as they progress through school and become more realistic about their college prospects.[43] Increasing college expectations by reducing the price and price uncertainty early on might therefore be precursors to behavioral changes and greater academic effort later in high school.[44]

The Canadian *Future to Discover* (FTD) program provides evidence that promise scholarships can increase social capital in just this way. This early aid program involved $8,000 "learning accounts" assigned at random to low- and middle-income students in Canada during tenth grade. Students "earned" $2,000 for each year of high school completed and for meeting attendance requirements. Students in the study were at or below the provincial median income.[45] Fowler and her colleagues note the program had positive effects on college expectations in the first two years, especially among students from families with low incomes and low parental education. Effects on high school academic outcomes are not reported.[46]

The above theory and evidence was instrumental not only in deciding that the program might represent a cost-effective improvement in the design of financial aid, but also, as a demonstration experiment, it informed some of the specific design decisions. Consider first that TDP starts in ninth grade and has more time to work, in contrast to FTD (tenth grade) and traditional aid (twelfth grade). Performance requirements, which are not included in many purely need-based programs, are fundamental to the design of TDP.[47] These include output-oriented performance requirements (GPA) and, as suggested by Fryer, school attendance as an input-oriented requirement. TDP provides reminders to students about the program and information so that they better understand what they need to accomplish to achieve college success.[48] To facilitate the role of peer effects and college-going culture, the entire cohort of first-time ninth graders in each school was selected, in contrast to all prior randomized trials of college aid which randomized individuals.[49] Finally, TDP does not require eligibility for Pell or any other grant, reducing the possibility that students might lose TDP for reasons outside their control.[50] It remains to be seen whether these design choices were sufficient to change how students think about college or what they do to prepare for it.

Potential implications for the nation's financial aid system

Given strong political support for financial aid, perhaps the most important policy question is whether early aid proves more cost effective than traditional late commitment aid. If it does, then shifting to an early aid approach could improve college access and address continued gaps in college outcomes. The primary benefits are the types of improved preparation studied here during students' high school years, while the costs are arguably small.[51] Even modest effects on high school preparation could be important given growing evidence that, as Heckman writes, skill begets skill.[52]

There are two main impediments, however, to revamping traditional aid with early commitments. First, it is not clear whether the government can credibly commit to providing funding many years in advance in the way the TDP funder did. One solution would be for the government to deposit the money into a bank account in the student's name when the funds are first committed as is done in the social security systems in countries, such as Chile. This not only largely eliminates the credible commitment problem but also takes advantage of the fact that people seem to respond more strongly to the prospect of losing something to the prospect of gaining that same thing—sometimes called "loss aversion."[53] Once the government puts the money in an account, students may fear losing it.

Even within a more typical pay-as-you-go-type system, the government could convince students the money will be there if they provide stable funding over time, a de facto commitment.[54] Indeed, the real level of total government grants for college has remained steady or grown every year since 1982.[55] The U.S. Social Security system is another case in point. Prior actions by governments are the best predictors of future actions.

A second impediment is that aid packages depend on the college attended and students do not know that in advance. Aside from eliminating the college-specific nature of aid, one solution to this problem would be to commit some minimum aid level that the government would provide no matter what college the student chooses. If the government could also simplify aid applications and link them to IRS records, then most students could receive their aid commitments from the government automatically when they enter ninth grade, for example, based on parent income at that point in time.

Government financial aid programs—which now spend $177 billion annually—have no doubt contributed to the growth of educational attainment over the past century.[56] But in an environment where government support for higher education will continue to be strained by health care, pensions, and other government responsibilities, it may be necessary to rethink the design of existing programs and allocation of higher education resources. Early aid may be one way to improve efficiency and equity simultaneously. Over the next several years, the potential benefits will become clearer as students in Milwaukee, Kalamazoo, and Canada progress through school and into the workforce.

Notes

1. Carneiro, P. M., & Heckman, J. J. (2003). Human capital policy. In J. J. Heckman & A. B. Krueger (Eds.), *Inequality in America: What role for human capital policies?* (pp. 77–240). Cambridge, MA: MIT Press; Haveman, R., & Wilson, K. (2007). Access, matriculation, and graduation. In S. Dickert-Conlin & R. Rubenstein (Eds.), *Economic inequality and higher education* (pp. 17–43). New York, NY: Russell Sage Foundation.

2. Bailey, M. J., & Dynarski, S. M. (2011). *Gains and gaps: Changing inequality in U.S. college entry and completion* (NBER Working Paper No. 17633). Cambridge, MA: National Bureau of Economic Research. School and college success also correlates highly with race. Only 65 percent of minority students even graduate from high school (Heckman & LaFontaine, 2007) and, of those, only a little over half go right on to some type of college (Aud et al., 2011).

3. Wolfe, B. L., & Haveman, R. H. (2003). Social and nonmarket benefits from education in an advanced economy. In Y. K. Kodrzycki (Ed.), *Education in the 21st century: Meeting the challenges of a changing world*, (pp. 97–131). Boston, MA: Federal Reserve Bank of Boston.

4. Adelman, C. (2006). *The toolbox revisited: Paths to degree completion from high school through college.* Washington, DC: U.S. Department of Education.

5. Reardon, S. F. (2012). The widening socioeconomic status achievement gap: New evidence and possible explanations. In R. Murnane & G. Duncan (Eds.), *Social and inequality and economic disadvantage* (pp. 91–116). Washington, DC: Brookings Institution.

6. Bailey & Dynarski (2011). ; Carneiro & Heckman (2003).

7. Goldin, C., & Katz, L. (2008). *The race between education and technology.* Cambridge, MA: Harvard University Press.

8. Ehrenberg, R. (2002). *Tuition rising.* Cambridge, MA: Harvard University Press; Geiger, R. & Heller, D. (2011). *Financial trends in higher education: The United States* (Working Paper No. 6). University Park, PA: Center for the Study of Higher Education, The Pennsylvania State University. Parents without college degrees have seen their real wages and incomes decline (U.S. Census, 1998; Mishel et al., 2012) and there was been essentially no real income growth in the bottom quintile during 1973–2005.

9. Geiger & Heller (2011).

10. College Board. (2012). *Trends in college pricing.* Retrieved May 3, 2013, from http://trends.collegeboard.org/sites/default/files/college-pricing-2012-full-report-121203.pdf.

11. Dynarksi, S. (2003). Does aid matter? Measuring the effect of student aid on college attendance and completion. *American Economic Review, 93*(1), 279–288; Goldin, & Katz (2008); Bowen, W. G., Chingos, M. M., & McPherson, M. (2009). *Crossing the finish line: Completing college at America's public*

universities. Princeton, NJ: Princeton University Press; Deming, D., & Dynarski, S. (2009). *Into college, out of poverty? Policies to increase the postsecondary attainment of the poor* (NBER Working Paper No. 15387). Retrieved from National Bureau of Economic Research website: http://www.nber.org/papers/w15387; Ikenberry, S. O., & Hartle, T. W. (1998). *Too Little knowledge is a dangerous thing: What the public thinks and knows about paying for college*. Washington, DC: American Council on Education.

12. Harris, D. N. (2013). Applying cost effectiveness analysis to higher education: A framework for improving productivity. In A. Kelly & K. Carey (Eds.), *Stretching the higher education dollar: How innovation can improve access, equity, and affordability* (pp. 45–66). Washington, DC: American Enterprise Institute.

13. Dynarski, S., & Scott-Clayton, J. (2006). The cost of complexity in federal student aid: Lessons from optimal tax theory and behavioral economics. *National Tax Journal, 59*(2), 319–356; Bettinger, E. P., Long, B. T., Oreopoulos, P., & Sanbonmatsu, L. (2009). *The role of simplification and information in college decisions: Results from the H&R Block FAFSA experiment* (NBER Working Paper No. 15361). Retrieved from National Bureau of Economic Research website: http://www.nber.org/papers/w15361

14. Economist. (2008, February 7). *Rescuing Kalamazoo: A promising future*. Economist, Retrieved from http://www.economist.com/node/10650702 (accessed March 1, 2012); Schwartzman, P. (2011, December 17). The promise: Two wealthy men set out to transform the lives of 59 fifth-graders. *Washington Post*. Retrieved from http://articles.washingtonpost.com/2011-12-17/local/35287524_1_seat-pleasant-elementary-william-smith-fifth-graders; Fishman, T. (2012, September 13). The tuition jackpot: Why these kids get a free ride to college. *New York Times Magazine*, p. MM38.

15. Obama, B. (2010, June 7). *Remarks by the President at Kalamazoo Central High School Commencement*. Retrieved March 1, 2013, from http://www.whitehouse.gov/the-press-office/remarks-president-kalamazoo-central-high-school-commencement

16. Author's calculations using National Student Clearinghouse data.

17. The $12,000 will come through their financial aid package at their chosen college. "On time" graduation means within four years of starting ninth grade.

18. Like almost all forms of college financial aid, receiving the funds requires that students be degree seeking and have at least $1 of unmet need. (Unmet need is the cost of attendance minus the expected family contribution and existing grant and scholarship aid (excluding loans and work study)).

19. Bowen et al. (2009); Roderick, M., Nagaoka, J., Coca, V., & Moeller, E. (2009). *From high school to the future: Making hard work pay off: The road to college for students in CPS's academically advanced programs*. Chicago, IL: Consortium for Chicago Schools Research; Rosenbaum, J. (2001). *Beyond college for all: Career paths for the forgotten half*. New York, NY: Russell Sage Foundation; Schneider, B., & Stevenson, D. (1999). *The ambitious generation: America's teenagers, motivated but directionless*. New Haven, CT: Yale University Press.

20. Fowler, H. S., Currie, S., Hébert, S., Kwakye, I., Ford, R., Hutchison, J., & Dobrer, S. (2009). *Future to discover: Interim impacts report*. Montreal, Quebec, Canada: Social Research and Demonstration Corporation. Retrieved from http://www.srdc.org/uploads/FTD_IIR_report_ENG.pdf

21. Bettinger et al. (2009).

22. There are some disadvantages of experiments, including their somewhat higher cost and the fact that program implementation and feedback effects are differ from more natural or scaled up programs. See, for example, Larsen, M. & Harris, D. N. (forthcoming). Experiments versus Quasi-Experiments. In D. Brewer & L. Picus (Eds.), *Encyclopedia of Education Economics and Education Finance*. Washington, DC: Sage Publications.

23. Bartik, T. J., Eberts, R., & Huang, W.-J. (2010, June). *The Kalamazoo promise, and enrollment and achievement trends in Kalamazoo Public Schools*. Paper presented at the PromiseNet 2010 Conference, Kalamazoo, MI.

24. While our randomization is an improvement on individual randomization, it does not mimic a real-world situation. For example, there are some non-first-time ninth graders in the TDP treatment schools and of course many 10th, 11th, and 12th graders. Also, some TDP students will transfer over time.

25. Nagaoka, J., Roderick, M., & Coca, V. (2008). *Barriers to college attainment: Lessons from Chicago*. Chicago, IL: Consortium for Chicago Schools Research.

26. Johnson, J., Rochkind, J. (with Ott, A. N., & DuPont S.) (2012). *With their whole lives ahead of them*, Reserach by Public Agenda. New York, NY: Bill & Melinda Gates Foundation.

27. Bowen et al. (2009).

28. Hoxby, C. M., & Avery, C. (2012) *The missing "One-Offs": The hidden supply of high-achieving, low income students caroline* (NBER Working Paper No. 18586). Cambridge, MA: National Bureau of Economic Research; Bowen et al. (2009); Roderick, M., Nagaoka, J., Coca, V., & Moeller, E. (2008). *From high school to the future: Potholes on the road to college*. Chicago, IL: Consortium for Chicago Schools Research.

29. Goldrick-Rab, S., Harris, D., & Trostel, P. (2009). Why financial aid matters (or does not) for college success: Toward a new interdisciplinary approach. In J. Smart (Ed.), *Higher education: Handbook of theory and research* (Vol. 24, pp. 1–45). New York, NY: Springer.

30. Manski, C. (1993). Adolescent econometricians: How do youth infer the returns to schooling? In C. Clotfelter & M. Rothschild (Eds.), *Studies of supply and demand in higher education* (pp. 43–57). Chicago, IL: University of Chicago Press; Manski (1993); Beattie, I. (2002). Are all 'adolescent econometricians' created equal? Racial, class and gender differences in college enrollment. *Sociology of Education, 75*(1), 19–43.

31. Adelman (2006).

32. Deming & Dynarski (2009); Angrist, J., Lang, D., & Oreopoulos, P. (2009). Incentives and services for college achievement: Evidence from a randomized trial. *American Economic Journal: Applied Economics, 1*(1), 1–28; Scott-Clayton, J. (2011). On money and motivation: A quasi-experimental

analysis of financial incentives for college achievement. *Journal of Human Resources*, *46*(3), 614–646.

33. Bartik et al. (2010); Miron, G., Spybrook, J., & Evergreen, S. (2008). *Key findings from the 2007 survey of high school students* (Evaluation of the Kalamazoo Promise: Working Paper No. 3). Retrieved from the Western Michigan University website: http://www.wmich.edu/leadership/kpromise/documents/studentsurvey-3.pdf

34. Miron, G., Jones, J. N., & Kelaher Young, A. J. (2009). *The impact of the Kalamazoo Promise on student attitudes, goals, and aspirations* (pp. 5–6) (Evaluation of the Kalamazoo Promise: Working Paper No. 6). Retrieved from the Western Michigan University website: https://www.wmich.edu/leadership/kpromise/documents/aspirations-6.pdf

35. Bartik, T., & Lachowska, M. (2011). *The short-term effects of the Kalamazoo promise scholarship on student outcomes*. Paper presented at the 2011 annual meeting of the Association for Public Policy and Management, Washington, DC.

36. Roderick et al. (2009).

37. Spielhagen, F. (2007). *Intersecting inequities: Examining the impact of early high school experiences on college admissions through the Texas Higher Education Opportunity Project* (Working Paper). Retrieved from Higher Education Opportunity Project website: http://theop.princeton.edu/publications/wp.asp

38. Harris, D. (2010). How do school peers influence student educational outcomes? Theory and evidence from economics and other social sciences. *Teachers College Record*, *112*(4), 1163–1197.

39. Hoxby, C. M., & Weingarth, G. (2005). *Taking race out of the equation: School reassignment and the structure of peer effects.* Unpublished manuscript, Harvard University, Cambridge, MA; Jencks, C., & Mayer, S. E. (1990). The social consequences of growing up in a poor neighborhood. In L. E. Lynn, Jr. & M. G. H. McGeary (Eds.), *Inner city poverty in the United States* (pp. 111–186). Washington, DC: National Academy Press; Harris (2010).

40. Roderick et al. (2009).

41. Gamoran, A., & Hannigan, E. C. (2000). Algebra for everyone? Benefits of college-preparatory mathematics for students of diverse abilities in early secondary school. *Educational Evaluation and Policy Analysis*, *22*(3), 241–254.

42. Ou, S., & Reynolds, A. J. (2008). Predictors of educational attainment in the Chicago Longitudinal Study. *School Psychology Quarterly*, *23*(2), 199–229.

43. Elliott, W. (2009). Children's college aspirations and expectations: The potential role of children's development accounts (CDAs). *Children and Youth Services Review*, *31*, 274–283; Reynolds, J. R., & Pemberton, J. (2001). Rising college expectations among youth in the United States: A comparison of the 1979 and 1997 NLSY. *The Journal of Human Resources*, *36*(4), 703–726; Cook, T. D., Church, M. B., Ajanaku, S., Shadish, W. R., Jr., Kim, J.-R., & Cohen, R. (1996). The development of occupational aspirations and expectations among inner-city boys. *Child Development*, *67*, 3368–3385; Trusty, J. (2000). High educational expectations

and low achievement: Stability of educational goals across adolescence. *Journal of Educational Research*, *93*, 356–365.

44. Student performance on standardized tests, for example, was influenced in one experiment by randomly assigned information meant to affect students' beliefs about their academic abilities.

45. Fowler et al. (2009).

46. Fowler et al. (2009).

47. Baum, S., Breneman, D., Chingos, M., Ehrenberg, R., Fowler, P., Hayek, J., ... Whitehurst, G. (2012). *Beyond need and merit: Strengthening state grant programs*. Washington, DC: Brookings Institution; Deming & Dynarski (2009).

48. Roderick et al. (2009).

49. Fletcher, J. M., & Tienda, M. (2009). High school classmates and college success. *Sociology of Education*, *82*(4), 287–314; Harris (2010); Spielhagen (2007).

50. Cite WSLS.

51. The primary cost is that some students who are initially eligible early in school may become ineligible once they reach college age, but still receive the scholarship funds.

52. Heckman, J. J. (2000). Policies to foster human capital. *Research in economics*, *54*(1), 3–56.

53. Fryer, R. G., Jr. (2010). *Financial incentives and student achievement: Evidence from randomized trials* (NBER Working Paper No. 15898). Retrieved from National Bureau of Economic Research website: http://www.nber.org/papers/w15898

54. Heller (2006) argues that stable funding is not enough because of the growth of tuition costs, but this growth itself has been predictable and this same problem arises with late commitment aid. He also provides evidence about the stability of eligibility over time. To ensure that students who fall into poor economic conditions toward the end of high school are still eligible for aid, students could always request that their aid packages be updated. This would have the side effect that, for any given level of funding, aid will be somewhat less well targeted to low-income families compared with late commitment aid; however, these differences are likely to be small given the stability of family circumstances.

55. Geiger & Heller (2011).

56. Goldin & Katz (2008).

DOUGLAS N. HARRIS *is an associate professor of economics and University Endowed Chair in Public Education at Tulane University.*

Index

Advise Texas experiment, 70; academic
    preparation, 107–108;
    affordability, 107
antonio, a. l., 2, 6, 55, 74
Arnold, K., 86
Associated Colleges of the Midwest
    (ACM), 49
"Attentional failure," 82

Bartik, T. J., 107, 108
Bettinger, E. P., 2, 6, 55, 56, 75, 87
Bowen, W., 32
Broda, M., 2, 3, 5, 9, 29
Burkander, K., 2, 3, 5, 9, 29

CAP. *See* College Ambition Program
    (CAP)
CAP center, 15, 20, 23
Carnegie Foundation for Teaching and
    Learning President Tony Bryk, 47
Castleman, B. L., 3, 7, 18, 77, 97
CCC. *See* College Counselors'
    Collaborative (CCC)
CCSR. *See* Consortium on Chicago
    School Research (CCSR)
Chester, M., 3
Chicago Postsecondary Transition
    Project, 35
Chicago Public Schools (CPS), 31–51;
    educational attainment in, 47;
    extensive data archive on, 35–37;
    students' college and FAFSA, 40
Chingos, M., 32
Coach model, for application process,
    14–15; advantages of, 14;
    functions of, 14
College Ambition Program (CAP),
    5–6, 15–27; activities of, 16;
    component of, 15; partnership
    with school counseling staff, 16;
    practical applications of, 26–27;
    preliminary findings of, 20–27;
    programmatic aspect of, 16;
    randomized microintervention,

19; special training program, 17;
    student perspectives, 22–26;
    student response to, 21; summer
    melt and, 17–21; support to
    low-income students, 16–17;
    sustainability of, 26–27
College application process, 13–15;
    assisting high school students in,
    13–15; coaches role in, 14
College Counselors' Collaborative
    (CCC), 48–50; job-embedded
    coaching and, 48; students'
    application activity and, 50
College enrollment, 43; low college
    completion and, 44; students with
    lower academic qualification and,
    43
College Goal Sunday, 83
College-going culture, 2–2; high
    school effects on, 33–34;
    qualitative approach, 69; scholarly
    studies, 69
College-going process, 1–2
College search/selection process, 10,
    11–13; advanced level courses and,
    11; complexity of, 11; institutional
    factors, 12; theory of action, 12;
    visualize as college student, 12;
    "undermatching", 12
Consortium on Chicago School
    Research (CCSR), 2, 6, 31;
    building knowledge of core
    problems, 45–47; capacity
    building research, 33–35; capacity
    of practitioners and, 35; CPS
    graduates issues and, 31–32; data
    tracking and, 37; information to
    broader audiences, 47; scientific
    research while making findings
    accessible, 40–44
Counselors, as social capital, 108
CPS graduates, 31–32; academic
    records of, 36
Current Population Survey, 32

117

The Degree Project (TDP), 8, 99–112;
   communications plan, 103;
   general rationale for, 105–110;
   implications for nation's financial
   aid system, 110–112; overview,
   99–101; random assignment, 104;
   scholarships, 102; social capital,
   108–110; "individual
   randomization", 104

Eberts, R., 107
Educational attainment, 31–33; and
   economic (in)security, 31; and
   social inequality, 31, 32
Evans, B. J., 2, 6, 55, 74

FAFSA. *See* Free Application for
   Federal Student Aid (FAFSA)
FCS. *See* Fulton County Schools (FCS)
Foster, J. D., 2, 6, 55, 74
Free Application for Federal, 102
Free Application for Federal Student
   Aid (FAFSA), 13, 16, 23, 47, 103;
   CPS students' college and, 40;
   filing, 38–40
From High School to the Future, 46
From High School to the Future:
   Potholes on the Road to College,
   38
From High School to the Future: The
   Challenge of Senior Year in
   Chicago Public Schools, 47
Fryer, R. G., Jr., 110
Fulton County Schools (FCS), 84;
   counselor, 84–85; FRL-eligible
   students in, 85
Future to Discover (FTD) program,
   109

Government financial aid programs,
   111
Group-based contagion, 108

Harris, D. N., 2, 8, 99, 116
Heckman, J. J., 110
High schools serving, 10; to
   low-income populations, 10; to
   middle- and high-income
   students, 10, 11

Holsapple, M., 2, 3, 6, 31, 53
Horng, E. L., 2, 3, 6, 55, 74
Huang, W.-J., 107
Hurd, N. F., 2, 6, 55, 75

Illinois Student Assistance Commission
   (ISAC), 40
"Individual randomization," 104
International Baccalaureate Program
   (IB, 24

Johnson, D. W., 2, 3, 6, 31, 53
Judy, J., 1, 2, 3, 5, 9, 29

Kalamazoo Promise, 101
Kalamkarian, H. S., 2, 6, 55, 75
Karlan, D., 82

Lachowska, M., 108
Long, B. T., 56, 87
Loss aversion, 111

Mastery Charter Schools, 90
McConnell, M., 82
McPherson, M., 32
Milwaukee Area Technical College
   (MATC), 102
Moeller, E., 2, 3, 6, 31, 53
Monetary Assistance Program (MAP)
   grants, 40
Mullainathan, S., 82

National College Advising Corps
   (NCAC), 2, 6, 55–74; college
   advising dosage experiment, 70;
   data-driven program changes,
   71–73; data sources, 57–62;
   adviser survey, 59; NSC data, 60;
   site visits, 60–61; student survey
   data, 58–59; triangulation of,
   61–62; difference-in-differences
   methodology, 66; overview, 55–57;
   partnerships program, 62–69;
   evaluation team and multilevel, 65;
   postsecondary institutions, 63;
   program design, 63–65; research
   relationships with individual
   states, 65–69; shared assumptions,

62; university-district-school, 64; scholarly studies, 69–71; advise Texas experiment, 70; college advising dosage experiment, 70; college-going culture, 69

National Science Foundation, 19

National Student Clearinghouse (NSC), 35, 58, 65; data from, 60

NCAC. *See* National College Advising Corps (NCAC)

NCS. *See* Network for College Success (NCS)

Network for College Success (NCS), 6

NSC. *See* National Student Clearinghouse (NSC)

Oreopoulos, P., 56

Owen, L., 87

Page, L. C., 3, 7, 77, 97

Peer mentoring, 89–90; to mitigate summer attrition, 89–90

Peer mentors, 90–92; counselor-led outreach interventions and, 91; goals for, 91; text messaging and, 92

Pittsburgh Promise, 102

Postsecondary attainment, for urban students, 32

Postsecondary enrollment rates, 22

Postsecondary tracking system, Chicago's, 36

Potholes report, 40, 46

Roderick, M., 48

Rosenbaum, J., 33

Sanbonmatsu, L., 56

Schneider, B., 1, 2, 3, 4, 5, 9, 12, 29

Schoolteachers, as social capital, 108

Science, technology, engineering, and mathematics (STEM) careers, 16, 22

Skelton, C., 3

Smartphones, in education, 19

Social capital, 108–110

STEM careers. *See* science, technology, engineering, and mathematics (STEM) careers

Stevenson, D., 12

Summer attrition, 78

"Summer fadeout," 77

Summer melt, 18; causes of, 79–83; mitigating, 83–88; overview, 77–79; peer mentoring to mitigate, 89–90; sites and intervention design, 90–94

Summer mentors, 18

TDP. *See* The Degree Project (TDP)

Teach For America (TFA), 14

The Teaching Fellows (TF), 14

Texas Higher Education Coordinating Board, 70

Text campaign, 91

Text messaging, 20–21; CAM and, 20–21; cost of, 93; and peer mentor outreach campaigns, 92; to deliver personalized college information, 88–89

uAspire, 84, 90, 93

University-district-school partnership, 64

University–community partnerships, 2–3; negative findings in, handling of, 3

Zinman, J., 82

NEW DIRECTIONS FOR YOUTH DEVELOPMENT

ORDER FORM SUBSCRIPTION AND SINGLE ISSUES

DISCOUNTED BACK ISSUES:

Use this form to receive 20% off all back issues of *New Directions for Youth Development*.
All single issues priced at **$23.20** (normally $29.00)

TITLE	ISSUE NO.	ISBN

Call 888-378-2537 or see mailing instructions below. When calling, mention the promotional code JBNND to receive your discount. For a complete list of issues, please visit www.josseybass.com/go/ndyd

SUBSCRIPTIONS: (1 YEAR, 4 ISSUES)

☐ New Order   ☐ Renewal

U.S.	☐ Individual: $89	☐ Institutional: $318
CANADA/MEXICO	☐ Individual: $89	☐ Institutional: $358
ALL OTHERS	☐ Individual: $113	☐ Institutional: $392

Call 888-378-2537 or see mailing and pricing instructions below.
Online subscriptions are available at www.onlinelibrary.wiley.com

ORDER TOTALS:

Issue / Subscription Amount: $ _____

Shipping Amount: $ _____
(for single issues only – subscription prices include shipping)

Total Amount: $ _____

SHIPPING CHARGES:	
First Item	$6.00
Each Add'l Item	$2.00

(No sales tax for U.S. subscriptions. Canadian residents, add GST for subscription orders. Individual rate subscriptions must be paid by personal check or credit card. Individual rate subscriptions may not be resold as library copies.)

BILLING & SHIPPING INFORMATION:

☐ **PAYMENT ENCLOSED:** *(U.S. check or money order only. All payments must be in U.S. dollars.)*

☐ **CREDIT CARD:** ☐ VISA ☐ MC ☐ AMEX

Card number _____ Exp. Date _____

Card Holder Name_____ Card Issue # _____

Signature _____ Day Phone _____

☐ **BILL ME:** *(U.S. institutional orders only. Purchase order required.)*

Purchase order # _____
Federal Tax ID 13559302 • GST 89102-8052

Name _____

Address_____

Phone_____ E-mail_____

Copy or detach page and send to: **John Wiley & Sons, One Montgomery Street, Suite 1200, San Francisco, CA 94104-4594**

Order Form can also be faxed to: **888-481-2665**

PROMO JBNND